Politics of Compromise:

NATO and AWACS

Politics of Compromise:
NATO and AWACS

Arnold Lee Tessmer

1988

 National Defense University Press
Washington, DC

NATIONAL DEFENSE UNIVERSITY PRESS PUBLICATIONS

To increase general knowledge and inform discussion, NDU Press publishes books on subjects relating to US national security.

Each year, in this effort, the National Defense University, through the Institute for National Strategic Studies, hosts about two dozen Senior Fellows who engage in original research on national security issues. NDU Press publishes the best of this research.

In addition, the Press publishes other especially timely or distinguished writing on national security, as well as new editions of out-of-print defense classics, and books based on University-sponsored conferences concerning national security affairs.

> Opinions, conclusions, and recommendations expressed or implied within are solely those of the author, and do not necessarily represent the views of the National Defense University, the Department of Defense, or any other US Government agency. This book is cleared for public release; distribution unlimited.

Portions of this book may be quoted or reprinted without permission, provided that a standard source credit line is included. NDU Press would appreciate a courtesy copy of reprints or reviews.

The manuscript of this book was word-processed under contract DAHC32-87-A-0013 by SSR, Inc., Washington, DC. This book was indexed under contract DAHC32-87-A-0017 by Editorial Research Associates.

NDU Press publications are sold by the US Government Printing Office. For ordering information, call (202) 783-3238 or write to the Superintendent of Documents, US Government Printing Office, Washington, DC 20402.

Library of Congress Cataloging in Publication Data
Tessmer, Arnold Lee.
    Politics of compromise: NATO and AWACS/Arnold Lee Tessmer. p. cm.
    Bibliography: p.
    Includes index.
    $7.50 (est.)
    1. North Atlantic Treaty Organization—Armed Forces—Procurement. 2. Electronic warfare aircraft—Europe. 3. Airborne warning and control systems. I. Title.
UG1125.E87T47 1988   88-17584
358.4'5—dc19   CIP

First printing June 1988

*Dedicated to my children
Jennifer, Eric, and Jeremy*

CONTENTS

Foreword   *xi*
Preface   *xiii*

1. A QUESTION OF AFFORDABILITY   *1*
   Cost and Value   *2*
   A First Proposal   *5*
   The Press of Time   *7*
   The Sales Campaign   *9*
   A Second Proposal   *13*
   Financial Negotiations
      Round One—First Session   *18*
   Round One—Second Session   *28*

2. THE NIMROD DECISION   *31*
   A Reluctant Choice   *31*
   Ministers in Extraordinary Session   *36*
   The Aftermath   *43*
   A Spate of New Proposals   *47*

3. THE SEARCH FOR CONSENSUS   *55*
   A Seminal Bilateral   *56*
   An Honest Broker   *61*
   Round Two—First Session   *63*
   Second Session—The Belgian Proposal   *69*
   Sessions Three and Four   *73*
   Round Two—A Final Session   *78*
   The Italian Amendment   *84*

4. UNCERTAINTIES   *89*
   A Precarious Beginning   *90*
   An Inherited Political Problem   *97*
   The Decision Document   *104*
   A Final Flurry   *111*

5. IN MINISTERIAL SESSION   *123*
    December 5th   *123*
    December 6th   *131*

6. AN IMPERFECT AGREEMENT?   *143*
    A First Test   *144*
    The Staggered Payments Schedule   *148*
    Termination Liability   *151*
    An Imperfect Agreement?   *154*

AUTHOR'S EPILOGUE   *159*

ENDNOTES   *165*
SELECTED BIBLIOGRAPHY   *201*
INDEX   *205*
THE AUTHOR   *213*

FOREWORD

By the early 1970s, the military leaders of the North Atlantic Treaty Organization (NATO) had identified the Airborne Warning and Control System (AWACS) as a Priority One requirement, a designation given to few NATO military needs. However, as Arnold Lee Tessmer writes in this detailed account, the decision as to AWACS *affordability* was up to elected officials in the NATO nations. Thus, from the beginning, NATO's acquisition of AWACS was both a military and political issue.

Although AWACS had impressive military capabilities, it carried a high price tag—$75 million per system and a total purchase cost of some $2 billion. Because no single NATO nation could afford to acquire AWACS, a collective purchase effort was imperative. A joint NATO effort of this magnitude was unprecedented and risky for those political leaders who argued for AWACS. Although NATO members eventually agreed on the need for an early warning system, they debated the priority that should be assigned to its acquisition. Wouldn't it be better, some asked, to purchase, say, another 3,000 tanks or 300 fighter aircraft at comparable cost? Others argued for different warning systems: Britain, for example, favored its "Nimrod," while Germany spoke briefly for its "A–300 airbus." All debated their shares of the cost. Which nations, they asked, would benefit the most militarily and economically? The debate concluded with an extraordinary meeting in December 1978 when, after two years of intense negotiations, NATO defense ministers agreed to acquire AWACS.

In a lively narrative, refreshingly free of technical jargon, Lee Tessmer chronicles the debate over NATO's acquisition of this controversial system. This book, however, does more than tell an intriguing story. As we enter an era of collective fiscal constraint, Tessmer's study of political compromise certainly captures useful lessons for similar cooperative defense ventures among allies.

BRADLEY C. HOSMER
Lieutenant General, US Air Force
President, National Defense
   University

PREFACE

On 6 December 1978—after two years of fairly intense negotiations capping nearly a decade of contemplation—defense ministers of the North Atlantic Alliance agreed to acquire the Airborne Warning and Control System, or AWACS. Never before in NATO's thirty-year history had governments agreed to pool resources to acquire a collectively owned and operated defense asset.

Incongruously perhaps, the merits of the aircraft itself seemed to count for little during those final negotiations. This is not to say the airplane, and its impressive radar surveillance, warning, and control capabilities, did not matter. It mattered a lot, if NATO were to maintain a viable air defense posture. But then air defense stood as only one of several areas in NATO's defense posture that needed strengthening. Why AWACS and not more or better tanks, ships, aircraft, artillery, ammunition, or reinforcement capabilities? Because once governments accepted AWACS as a genuine test of political solidarity, failure to act would have carried more meaning—in terms of the very real political dimension of deterrence—than the agreement to proceed. Moreover, AWACS was a relatively "safe" initiative. It could not be pictured easily as a destabilizing, provocative move, such as, for example, the decision to deploy improved theater nuclear forces on European soil.

How NATO faced, and passed, this self-imposed test offers a particularly revealing look at the politics of compromise among coalition partners. That the airplane is both expensive (some two billion dollars in acquisition costs alone) and more than a bit controversial (nominated, for example, by Representative Patricia Schroeder (D-Colo.) in 1976 as "turkey of the year") suggests the breadth and depth of the compromise process. And that the United States Air Force AWACS—deployed to Northeast Asia when Korea's President Park was assassinated, to Saudi Arabia during the Iran-Iraq conflict, and to Europe during Poland's crisis—have become the modern-day equivalent of Theodore Roosevelt's great white fleet adds a measure of relevance to these compromises.

Unprecedented and relevant to current events though it may be, the NATO AWACS program does not lend itself easily to compact yet comprehensive treatment. The very richness of the story tempts overindulgence. It features a large and diverse case of principals and aides from all NATO capitals, and spans many changes in governments. It demonstrates quite clearly, for example, how important political decisions can be taken, or not taken, for reasons quite irrelevant to the merits of the issue. Thus we find the AWACS decision stalled in one capital in part because of the personal political ambitions of a defense minister, delayed in another because of almost irreconcilable language and religious differences, rejected in a third because of nationalistic pressures, and ignored in a fourth in part because a disgraced defense minister faced a jail term.

To bound the subject, therefore, this study centers on the two-year period (1977 and 1978) preceding defense ministers' approval of the program. However, to offer relative completeness and currency, it does treat key events before and after ministers' approval. To define it further, this study centers on the politics of the program as opposed to, say, the hardware or military aspects of the airplane. Yet, it touches on these and other subjects when necessary for a fuller treatment of political events. Above all else, it focuses on the process, details, and motivation in a narrow instance of give and take between allied governments with similar but decidedly different interests and values. To keep the study thus focused, I have placed many explanations and details in notes at the end of the book.

Few published materials analyze the NATO AWACS program. Public accounts of the program, lodged principally in the *Congressional Record*, do not document the decision-making process, only its more obvious results. Newspapers and magazines, even those specializing in NATO or defense matters, sketch only the vague outline of the story, and more of these than not are a notch out of focus. Moreover, much of the information harboring useful insights on the decision process was originally classified to protect national and Alliance security interests or, in a few cases, negotiating positions. The United States Department of Defense has, however, graciously disclosed portions of a few for this study. To flesh out the story behind the few written materials available, I have relied heavily on personal interviews with defense officials close to the program.*

---

*I interviewed senior officials in the American, British, German, and Italian defense establishments, among others. The bibliography details a complete listing.

Each person interviewed set his own rules. Some consented to candid exchanges only if their remarks were not attributed—but most opted for candor and attribution. In either case, I verified the information with other sources whenever possible, and it was possible in most instances. These recollections yielded a core story marked by consistency, plausibility, and relevance to national and Alliance security interests. In those few instances of inconsistent views or facts, I have offered a judgment, analysis, or contrast.

This case study of NATO's political machinery may be incomplete because it offers no conclusions, only insights into how a single, unprecedented, and costly NATO-wide initiative succeeded—despite obstacles, critics, and setbacks. Nevertheless, it should be valuable to students searching for a different perspective and to practitioners embarking on the uncertain course of securing NATO-wide agreement on another initiative affecting national treasuries.

This study is incomplete in other ways as well. Limits on funds and time available for research did not permit travel to all NATO capitals. Faced with having to make choices, I focused on the major contributors to the program: Canada, Germany, Italy, the United Kingdom, and the United States. The full story behind other governments' decisions to participate (Belgium, Denmark, Greece, Luxembourg, the Netherlands, Norway, Portugal, and Turkey) is no doubt just as revealing, and certainly just as important to a better understanding and appreciation of political compromise in NATO. I have therefore included as many of the known details behind the decision processes in this latter group of governments as could be reliably gathered without personal interviews. The reader, of course, will judge whether the results are adequate.

A thank you hardly seems fair recompense to all who helped with the content of this study. To the Honorable Frederick Mulley, who lingered over tea in the House of Commons to relate the internal and external pressures he faced as a defense minister, and to Herr Georg Leber, who halted his rush between Bundestag committee meetings to share an hour and his recollections as Minister of Defense, I owe a special and humble thanks. To General Dr. Karl Schnell, who opened his home and private papers and overwhelmed me with European hospitality, I owe a warm and enduring thank you.

Others were as generous. General Fabio Moizo agreed to drive more than an hour each way to a working lunch, and General Wolfgang Altenburg came in from winter maneuvers near Koblenz still wearing field gear. General Richard Bowman gave me free rein and office space in the Pentagon. Messrs. John Walsh and James Siena spent hours commenting on and improving an early draft, and countless Allied staff officers filled in the nooks and crannies of this work with important details.

I also owe a heartfelt thank you to a host of others responsible for this study. High on the list are the staff and editors of the National Defense University's Research Directorate, a professional lot with endless patience. Higher still is the long-forgotten military staff officer who sold the Chiefs of the United States Armed Services on the merits of the Research Fellowship program. It has been a unique opportunity for me.

To all, I owe a debt I hope is repaid in small measure by faithful reporting and fair analysis.

ARNOLD LEE TESSMER

Politics of
Compromise:

NATO and AWACS

Photo courtesy of the Boeing Company.
Used by permission.

A technician is dwarfed by the radome of the aircraft bearing the Airborne Warning and Control System (AWACS). The radome rotates every 10 seconds, providing 360 degree radar surveillance about the aircraft. This sophisticated warning and control capability made AWACS attractive from a military standpoint, but presented an imposing affordability problem to NATO.

1. A QUESTION OF AFFORDABILITY

In mid-1976, NATO's defense ministers concluded without much debate that governments could not afford the force of AWACS their senior military advisors said they needed to shore up Alliance defenses. No one should have been surprised, because all parties had played their traditional roles with predictable results.

Senior decision makers routinely challenge the affordability of military equipment for sound reasons. Faced with limited resources and what must seem like unlimited needs in a high-stakes contest, they must try to choose correctly between "necessary," "important," and "technologically possible" improvements in military capability. Such choices are seldom obvious and never easy.

The military community, unless pressed, tends to offer little help since, by its definitions, the armed forces seek only necessary improvements. Consequently, decision makers' challenges also serve as a sounding board. If, in response, the military community produces advocates who step forward with persistent, well-reasoned arguments, then the improvements may be necessary and, by extension, perhaps affordable. However perplexing this ritual of challenge and response may be to its participants—and however foolish the ritual may make Western defense establishments appear to the taxpaying public—decision makers rely on it to reduce the margin for wrong choices. Right and wrong choices, of course, remain a matter of opinion.

In this context alone, the NATO AWACS initiative simply could not have succeeded in 1976. But defense ministers did, in effect, give the military community a chance to argue AWACS' affordability, to prove its value warranted its cost. As it happened, NATO's military community chose not to argue the proposition. That unhappy role fell to the Americans and British.

Thus began a two-year struggle to define an affordable program—to reconcile cost and value to the satisfaction of thirteen sovereign governments, each with a different set of priorities and problems and a different sense of affordability. The effort not only shaped the form and substance of the NATO AWACS programs, it also tested the Alliance and member states in countless other important ways. Consider the affordability question first in general terms.

Cost and Value

Cost has plagued AWACS since its beginning over a decade ago. By any commonly used measure, it stacked up, at roughly $75 million a copy, as an extraordinarily expensive airplane.[1] High cost, particularly high unit cost, carried with it two important implications. First, high cost sustained the notion of a collective acquisition effort.[2] The aircraft was too expensive for any but a few allied governments to buy, let alone operate and maintain, whether that be one, two, or five (or whatever a fair share of NATO's requirements might be) and then to dedicate to the common defense, as was the practice with all other nationally owned weapons systems. Second, high price implies political cost. Few elected leaders in democratic political systems can afford the risk of seeking funds for $75 million airplanes without a convincing argument for backbenchers and the electorate.

The military value of AWACS was neither sufficiently compelling, nor well enough understood, to comprise the convincing argument needed during the early efforts to put together a NATO-wide program. Even if its military value had been in sharper focus, national decision makers still would have had to decide whether they needed AWACS more than they needed to fill shortages in other kinds of military equipment.

European leaders needed but to glance at how elements of the United States Congress reacted to AWACS to foresee how they might fare before their own legislatures. Using General Accounting Office reports as a cutting edge, congressional critics moved time and again to scuttle or delay the program, arguing that it cost too much, particularly for what it could add to battle management.[3] Calling it an airplane looking for a mission, critics claimed that the right kind of electronics countermeasures could render it useless, and that it was vulnerable to air and ground attacks. Tests, they declared, had not demonstrated its effectiveness in central Europe. The United States AWACS program limped ahead despite its critics, but at a financial and political price. Unit costs surged because of delays and changes in production schedules, and political costs, more difficult to measure, may have been equally high. AWACS, for years, bore the label of questionable utility and uncertain value before it was vindicated.

Value, after all, is a matter of opinion. Would a force of AWACS prove relatively more valuable to NATO's equipment-deficient deterrent posture than, say, another 3,000 tanks or 300 fighter aircraft at comparable cost? Once the need for a given military capability has been established, choices between weapons to satisfy that need are relatively simple, while choices between dissimilar weapons to satisfy dissimilar needs resist traditional analysis. Judgment, tempered as much by experience and vision as the analysts' findings, invariably illuminates the choice. Few would offer that kind of subjective judgment in favor of AWACS.[4]

NATO's Military Committee did stamp its imprimatur on AWACS, and, indeed, identified it as a priority-one requirement.[5] Although this value judgment stood indisputably as a necessary condition for NATO AWACS to move from concept toward reality, it remained an insufficient one. The judgment implied a choice only in the broad sense that the Military Committee accorded priority-one status to but few of many requirements. Put another way, the Military Committee, although blind neither to budget limitations nor to political realities, properly decides questions on the basis of military imperatives. Elected officials decide questions of affordability.

Therein lay the rub. NATO's political leadership, handicapped by an imperfect understanding of the AWAC's relative worth, nevertheless had to come to grips with accommodating its high cost within national defense budgets already limited by other national priorities and strained by other long-term defense initiatives. NATO's corporate military advisors endorsed it, but would not—could not within the confines of NATO's institutional arrangements—propose a trade-off that might have given elected leaders a sense of its value. The choices had to be taken in each capital where the question of affordability would be answered in a context peculiar to each government, and where the question would be subject to the political vagaries of the moment.

A First Proposal

Against this backdrop of general observations, one can better understand early failures with the NATO AWACS initiative. Working largely unfettered by political guidance on affordability—though with a political endorsement to develop a specific proposal—NATO's corporate military planners pieced together a recommended program calling for thirty-two specially configured AWACS (and associated support facilities) at an estimated cost somewhat above $3 billion. To state simply and without explanation that NATO defense ministers rejected the proposal out of hand as unaffordable (which they did in June 1976) would unfairly impugn the judgment that went into the proposal.

Consider the problem. NATO's unified air defense network (on which, by conventional wisdom, the favorable outcome of the first days of an attack from the East so much depends) is keyed to a string of ground radar surveillance and control sites built in the 1960s. These sites, however well exercised from years of air defense tests, simply cannot overcome their inherent limitations against aircraft flying at extremely low altitudes.[6] Although long aware of this deficiency, NATO's military experts did not cite the shortcoming as serious until 1970—at about the time the Soviets began producing attack aircraft with a more-than-theoretical low level attack capability. After a five-year effort by the NATO staff to focus attention on the problem, defense ministers directed authorities in 1975 to define a specific solution centering on AWACS.

"How much is enough?" "Enough"—whether derived from analysis, contemplation, or running a force development simulation through high speed computers—invariably turns on the planning assumptions employed. Planning assumptions, as any analyst or victim of the analytical arts knows, seem to border on the occult because they can make a problem disappear or multiply tenfold.[7] NATO's military planners, well aware of Allies' sensitivities to cost, used optimistic planning assumptions to derive the need for thirty-two AWACS. However, they simultaneously signalled that a lesser force, if that were all budgets would allow, could still improve NATO's defense posture. Bets were properly hedged.

Unaffordability, therefore, resulted less from untoward planning assumptions and recommended force levels than from other "facts of life." For reasons of technology transfer, balance-of-payments accounts, and jobs, some governments insisted that their industries help manufacture the system even though such arrangements would increase program costs by 10 percent. Some governments insisted on upgrading the system's capabilities at cost increases ranging as high as 15 percent. Fixed costs (as well as unit acquisition costs) were high. Probably most important, Allies' defense budgets, already committed to other programs, understandably held little slack for an unanticipated acquisition effort as expensive as AWACS. And, of course, many still challenged the relative worth of the program.

Each of these "facts," discussed in greater detail throughout this study, represented obstacles to program approval. At the same time, a host of other equally contentious acquisition arrangements (including, as just two examples, national cost shares and payment schedules) awaited negotiation. Moreover, all arrangements save contractual ones needed to be captured in decision documents that NATO's high councils could approve and forward to capitals for ratification. The effort required was, in a phrase, mind-boggling—particularly since two different sets of circumstances dictated an early decision by ministers.

The Press of Time

NATO moves at deliberate speed—always slower than some like, always faster than others prefer. But, in an alliance in which unanimity reigns as first principle, consensus tends to emerge at or near the pace of the most recalcitrant partner. As it turned out, this pretty much was the case for AWACS, although both the United Kingdom and the United States did their best to quicken the pace.

The United Kingdom pressed hard for an early decision by Allies because it faced an early choice between AWACS or a national system. Believers in early warning radar ever since it helped turn the tide during the Battle of Britain, the Ministry of Defence had begun in the mid-1960s a research program on advanced airborne radar. By 1973, the program had progressed far enough for the Ministry to wedge into its budget plans sufficient money to begin replacing the nearly obsolescent force of Shackleton Airborne Early Warning aircraft operated by the Royal Air Force.[8] Ministry officials originally set the sums to buy either nine AWACS or eleven Nimrod to replace Shackleton. They quietly dropped the AWACS option in favor of a NATO AWACS cost share, when that initiative seemed to hold promise, but also hedged against NATO AWACS not succeeding by starting development of a national system.

In mid-1976, the national program, Nimrod, had reached a point in research and development at which it needed either heftier slices of funding to continue in an efficient manner or termination in favor of a NATO-wide AWACS program. Her Majesty's Government preferred the AWACS option, but required a timely decision if it were to field a replacement for Shackleton in time. More will be said in the next chapter; the point here is that the British exigency largely paced events through early 1977.

Undoubtedly pleased to have the United Kingdom share some of the criticism heaped on frontrunners by less enthusiastic Allies, American defense officials' interest in an early decision was nonetheless acute and their drive to that point equally intense. Congress set the tempo. In 1975 and again in 1976, the Senate Armed Services Committee firmly decreed that the United States needed only twenty-one to twenty-four AWACS, including its share of a NATO program, rather than the thirty-four sought by the Department of Defense.[9] At then existing and projected production rates, the limit set by the Senate would have been reached in the Ford administration's Fiscal Year 1978 budget request. Subtracting production lead times from this date yielded a "no-later-than" decision point of about mid-1977 for the NATO program if a break in the production line, and its attendant cost penalty, were to be avoided. High costs already posed a problem for NATO, and still higher costs from restarting the production line would effectively foreclose NATO's decision to buy. Moreover, elements of both houses of the Congress so adamantly opposed AWACS that American defense officials could not be certain that even the 1977 "deadline" would hold.[10]

Thus, when defense ministers rejected the June 1976 proposal for thirty-two AWACS, British and American defense officials had reason for concern. The United Kingdom openly warned allies that a decision had to come by year's end. For its part the United States stepped up efforts to secure broader support for the program. The time had arrived for horse trading and, some would say, the polite arm twisting that had punctuated America's relations with Europe for more than a decade.

The Sales Campaign

While NATO's staff officials fretted over an alternative, less expensive proposal, the United States worked behind the scenes on a major sales campaign. The campaign, devised and implemented largely by the American Air Force,[11] called for three mutually supporting approaches: (1) build support for NATO AWACS in national defense establishments to which national political leaders, including those in legislatures, would turn at the appropriate moment for a professional assessment of the system's military value; (2) request the State Department to instruct American Ambassadors to relay to European Ministers of Foreign Affairs and Defense an explicit message that the United States Government (not just the Department of Defense) attached great importance to an early decision on NATO AWACS; and (3) undertake bilateral bargaining initiatives with Canada, the Federal Republic of Germany, and the United Kingdom, without whose collective support and major financial contributions the program would most assuredly fail. Each of these approaches attempted to change governments' views of AWACS' affordability by promoting its value. Apparently, no one thought to try to reduce costs.

These approaches, succeeding in some respects and failing in others, did capture attention in capitals. Grumbling about America's "hard sell" tactics lingered long after the campaign had ended. Consider first the two clear successes in Canada and the Netherlands. Each imparted much-needed momentum to a flagging initiative.

The approach to Canada yielded handsome results for both sides. The United States offered certain inducements if Canada would agree to entertain a significant share—something on the order of $200 to $250 million—of NATO AWACS costs. For Canada, whose annual defense budget at the time approximated $3.6 billion, the share proposed could be fairly characterized as extraordinary. It amounted, by way of rough comparison, to the funding efforts proposed for the United States' B-1 or M-X programs. When viewed in this context, American inducements, however generous they may have seemed to critics, were not excessive, and, one could argue, as advantageous to the United States as to Canada:

- Canadian defense industries would be awarded contracts valued at $60 to $70 million for manufacturing system components for NATO AWACS, provided their bids were in a competitive range and acceptable to all parties.
- That part of Canada's cost share spent in the United States for NATO AWACS would be counted against the Defense Production Sharing Agreement.[12]
- United States Air Force AWACS, flying North American air defense missions with Canadian participation, would provide surveillance (and, not incidentally, early warning for in-depth protection of American air space) at no capital investment cost to Canada. Canada would, however, pay some yet-to-be negotiated share of the operating and maintenance costs for such missions.[13]

The sales campaign also succeeded with the Netherlands. Its previous lack of enthusiasm for the program centered as much on doubts about the specific need for AWACS as on cost. The Netherlands' senior military shared the Military Committee's conclusion that deficiencies in the existing radar surveillance and control network would soon be intolerable, but doubted that AWACS offered the most cost effective alternative. Accordingly, the United States Air Force released an analytical study that demonstrated, at least to Dutch satisfaction, the relative cost superiority of AWACS in a European air campaign.[14] Straightaway, the Dutch warmed to the system and to the NATO program. The Dutch would find money for their share. The Netherlands, never anyone's shill in Alliance matters, emerged as the unofficial leader of the "minor-share" nations.[15] Its support proved significant.

The sales campaign enjoyed other, although less dramatic, successes as well. Campaign architects seized on the theme of political solidarity and raised it to the level of an almost compelling rallying cry. The campaign also succeeded in increasing several-fold European appreciation for the system's formidable capabilities. Before the campaign ended in early 1978, the commander of the United States AWACS wing met with, at their request, senior political and military leaders in all but three NATO capitals to detail for them a tactical commander's view of what AWACS could add to air battle management.[16] It was the perfect touch: no sales pitch, no gimmicks, no politics—just a solid, impressive presentation of information by an able commander. American embassies' reporting cables glowed with positive reactions.

The United States Air Force passed up no opportunity to demonstrate the system. While in Europe for operational tests, a single AWACS beamed its sweeping view of air traffic throughout central Europe simultaneously to selected (and duly impressed) audiences in three locations. On another occasion, when the German Defense Minister, Georg Leber, arrived in early March 1977 for consultations with the newly appointed Secretary of Defense, Harold Brown, the Air Force managed to have an AWACS and tons of support equipment waiting for him. General David C. Jones, then Air Force Chief of Staff and the leading advocate of the system, presided. Leber was delighted and, more to the point, impressed to the threshold of conversion from resigned participant to open advocate.

But the sales campaign fell short in some cases. It did not move the Germans (nor the Italians, Belgians, and perhaps others, but especially the Germans) rapidly or far enough to meet Britain's somewhat rigid timetable. As subsequent events would demonstrate, there simply was no way it could have. The campaign also led to the unintended conclusion in some capitals that the Americans might go to great lengths to secure the NATO program. They were right, but for the wrong reason. Conviction, not desperation, inspired the campaign.

A Second Proposal

By October 1976 the NATO staff had completed its revision of the proposal rejected by ministers as unaffordable four months earlier. Among other changes to the program, the revised proposal reduced estimated costs by about $600 million.

- Five aircraft were dropped from the program at a savings of roughly $300 million. The Military Committee, individual members having spent a professional lifetime getting by with less, agreed without conceding that force level requirements had changed.
- Certain European-preferred enhancements to the system's capabilities were deleted or deferred at a savings of another $300 million. The Military Committee acceded, with reservations.

The NATO staff well recognized that the revised proposal, although now less expensive and perhaps even affordable, retained serious flaws. Time would reveal their full extent, but at that moment cost-sharing arrangements stood as a known and imposing obstacle since, obviously, each government would weigh its cost share against its sense of AWACS' value. Most governments had rejected earlier attempts to allocate AWACS acquisition shares on the basis of NATO's existing burden-sharing formulas. Projects and activities funded by these existing formulas, over time and with a few tolerable exceptions, roughly balanced economic costs and benefits for each contributor. Application of these formulas to NATO AWACS would not have resulted in such a balance. The NATO staff tinkered with the traditional formulas to achieve a better balance between cost and benefits for participating governments, but neither the arithmetic nor politics of their variations would work. Relative to costs and benefits, particularly with the varied perceptions of that elusive quality "value" folded into the equation, the United Kingdom's and the United States' shares remain too low and Germany's too high.

The staff fed the proposal into NATO's decision-making machinery anyway—not because of any mindless optimism that ministers would sweep aside all remaining issues, but because they had gone as far as they could in the time allotted by circumstances.[17] They had largely met ministers' directions to relate force size, aircraft configuration, and industrial collaboration to the funding levels likely to be available. That the staff had failed so far to allocate acceptably the revised funding level among governments did not necessarily mean defense ministers would reject the program. Being closer to affordability counted for something. Besides, with a bit more of a kind of momentum created by Canada's and the Netherlands' newly won support combining with the United States' influence in capitals, differences might melt away when ministers addressed the task. Given the mounting political stakes, it would be altogether proper that ministers decide the question—whether cost and value meshed.

Unlikely as it seems in retrospect, perhaps they would have, had fate not introduced a new element of uncertainty to a program already brimming with that. Jimmy Carter, then generally unknown to Europeans, had centered his successful campaign on reforming the government, on realigning national priorities, and on eliminating the "$5 to $7 billion in waste" from the defense budget. Look at it from a European's perspective. Was NATO AWACS a Republican hobbyhorse that would fade away in the new administration? Congressional critics of the United States' AWACS program were mostly liberal Democrats.[18] Was not Carter a liberal Democrat? When defense ministers met on 7 December 1976, few present could have divined the answers.

For the Federal Republic of Germany in particular, an American lame-duck secretary of defense represented just one more reason why an agreement on AWACS was not in the cards. Leber himself lay at home recuperating from an appendectomy, thereby foreclosing whatever authority and flexibility he might have brought as a minister and senior German cabinet officer to the Defense Planning Committee meeting. His stand-in, Germany's ambassador to NATO Rolf Pauls, would be limited in substance to the position detailed in instructions from Bonn. Those instructions? Support the requirement for AWACS but do not commit the Federal Republic to any financial obligations or decision timetables. Point out that the newly elected Bundestag would not convene until mid-January and that German participation could hardly be its first order of business.[19]

Pauls' instructions reflected realities in Bonn that went well beyond legislative calendars and legislative priorities. Chancellor Helmut Schmidt had, on 30 March earlier that year, agreed privately to Germany's participation in NATO AWACS on the twin conditions that it be an Alliance-wide program and not require an increase in Germany's defense budget.[20] The latter requirement ensured conflict—and, as an inevitable consequence, delay—within the Ministry of Defense since the military services would understandably resist having their programs disrupted to accommodate AWACS. As will be seen, it would take time, persuasion, and economic offsets to mollify the opposition. At the moment, however, Pauls did not need instructions to know that Germany simply was not prepared to pay more than the United Kingdom and nearly as much as the United States for so little return. Pauls must have known, too, that Bonn still smarted over America's footdragging on evaluating the Leopard II tank to meet the American Army's main battle tank requirement.[21]

The ministers' discussions quickly dismissed any notion that the AWACS initiative would carry the day, but they more than kept it alive.[22] Some national positions played as predicted. The British Secretary of State for Defence, Frederick Mulley, called for an immediate decision. Secretary of Defense Donald Rumsfeld, who by Mulley's suggestion and prior arrangements with NATO Secretary General Joseph M. A. H. Luns, had spoken first to the need for AWACS, urged an early decision. Pauls did as he had been instructed.

Minister of National Defence Barnett Danson of Canada stood solidly in favor of the program. Other remarks were less predictable. Minister Vredeling, while not quite embracing an aircraft acquisition share, expressed the Netherland's surprisingly firm support for AWACS. Ambassador Marcel Fischbach of Luxembourg all but accepted the proposed cost-sharing arrangements. Minister Paul Vanden Boeynants of Belgium offered an impassioned plea, but limited funding, for the program. Portuguese Defense Minister Miquel accepted the proposal in principle without pledging a share. Vito Lattanzio, Italy's Minister of Defense, took pains to describe his country's poor economic condition while expressing reservations about the availability of surveillance coverage for the southern flank. Feyzioglu of Turkey accepted the proposal in principle, but reserved his government's position on cost sharing and tied that position to the location of a forward operating base in Turkey. Minister of Defense Rolf Hansen relayed Norway's positive, but not yet formal, support for the proposed cost-sharing arrangements, and Ambassador Anker Svart from Denmark clearly implied that his government would find a way to pay its dues. France, having withdrawn from the military organizations of NATO in 1966, had earlier sent its "no to acquisition, maybe to support costs" reply to Secretary General Luns who read it aloud for the record. Greece, unrepresented in the Defense Planning Committee for the twenty-eight months since it withdrew from NATO's integrated military structure over the crisis in Cyprus, had not signalled its position on the program.

A subsequent communique painted the meeting, in the bland colors peculiar to communiques, as a non-event:

> Ministers reaffirmed the importance of a NATO Airborne Early Warning Force and agreed to the need for an urgent decision of its realization. They therefore agreed to call a meeting of high-level national experts in early January in order to examine the financial aspects of such a realization, to be followed shortly thereafter by a meeting of Defense Ministers to come to decisions for endorsement through national processes. In the meantime operational implications are being discussed within the appropriate bodies.[23]

In reality, the program had lurched forward. Marching to the cadence sounded by a British tocsin, defense ministers had agreed to convene immediately a meeting of national financial experts under the auspices of Permanent Representatives to hammer out an agreement on cost sharing and other financial issues. They further agreed to reconvene the Defense Planning Committee in ministerial session as soon as practicable to decide on the financial experts' recommendations.

Cynics delight in pointing out that a call for meetings substitutes for action in NATO, but the alternative suggests a political arrangement inimical to the very soul of the most remarkable democratic alliance in history. How else do sovereign nation states, among whom countless disagreements in decades past were settled by the sword, forge a common stand?

Financial Negotiations Round One—
First Session

National financial experts gathered in Brussels on 11 January 1977. Governments' choices of representatives proved revealing. Consider some key examples (emphasis added to their government positions to underscore differences in background and perspective):

- John F. Anderson, then Chief of *Policy Plans* in the Ministry of National Defence—a disarmingly affable and shrewd negotiator who appeared equally comfortable with both price and value, whether gauged in political or economic terms—represented Canada.
- Dr. Hans Padberg, the organizational equivalent of *Comptroller* for the Federal Ministry of Defense—a man to whom logic and a sense of fairness appeared paramount and who, it appeared, could recite without hesitation costs and schedules for every new and projected piece of equipment in the Bundeswehr inventory—represented the Federal Republic of Germany.
- John Blelloch, then Assistant Under Secretary of State Aircraft in the office of the Defence Ministry's *Procurement Executive*, the archetypical British negotiator—with an extemporaneous eloquence capable of masking substance, a sense of fairness bounded by conscience and service to the Crown, and a master of the subject—represented the United Kingdom.
- Dale Babione, then acting Assistant Secretary of Defense for *Installations and Logistics*—a career civil servant whose rise in the Department of Defense was no doubt boosted by his reputation as one of the government's toughest contract negotiators—represented the United States.

20 A QUESTION OF AFFORDABILITY

Representatives from other governments were equally diverse and able. Most sensed, however, that their role would remain relatively low key until the major contributors edged closer to an accommodation of differences. NATO's Assistant Secretary General for Defence Support, Walter B. LaBerge, chaired the proceedings.

LaBerge himself had a hand in devising the cost-sharing proposal now before national financial experts. By dividing potential contributors into two groups he took the first step toward redressing the cost-benefit inequities that resulted from the application of more traditional cost-sharing formulas. The first group, comprising Canada, Germany, the United Kingdom, and the United States, would pay the bulk of aircraft acquisition costs in return for the bulk of economic and technology transfer benefits, while the second would pay half shares in return for reduced benefits. France and Greece, because neither participated in NATO's military structure, would be assigned arbitrary percentage shares. (This despite France's note to Secretary General Luns that it could not share acquisition costs.) LaBerge's compromise proposal yielded the following approximate cost shares (all figures expressed in US dollars):[24]

	$ Million		$ Million
Belgium	60	Luxembourg	2
Canada	180	Netherlands	60
Denmark	40	Norway	30
France	250	Portugal	5
Germany	615	Turkey	20
Greece	5	United Kingdom	450
Italy	100	United States	670

The preceding illustration hints at the core of Germany's problem with the cost-sharing proposal. For a share of $450 million, the United Kingdom would receive $150 million in industrial collaboration benefits *plus* long term economic and military benefits from hosting the AWACS main operating base. Over time, the British share stood to be completely amortized. For a share of $670 million, the United States could receive balance-of-payments benefits amounting to as much as $1.9 billion. That the United States offered to forgo most, if not perhaps all, pro rata recoupment charges for its more than $1 billion investment in AWACS research and development mitigated the apparent inequity somewhat but not enough. Sunk costs (previous investments) lend little leverage in such negotiations.

The Federal Republic's $615 million acquisition share would net perhaps a $200 million return. Moreover, if France held to its position, and powerful political precedents suggested that it would, the disparity between costs and benefits promised to get only worse. Where would the money come from? Granted other European governments—save the United Kingdom, a special case—had fully obligated their respective defense budgets for the next five years and would therefore have to dislocate national defense programs to accommodate AWACS, how could Germany's defense budget accommodate a $600 million dislocation? What would go: Leopard II tanks, frigates, Multi-Role Combat Aircraft?

A defense budget supplement was possible of course, but Schmidt's Social Democrats—having pledged during the previous fall's election campaign not to increase defense spending—would expect a convincing argument. What would it be? AWACS could hardly pass as the ultimate deterrent worth any sacrifice. Yes, it could offer precious minutes' additional warning of a sneak air attack, sort out feints from thrusts, and multiply the lethality of air defense systems. It might also impel weapons standardization from concept toward reality, and certainly it testified to Alliance solidarity. But what could AWACS do, the Bundestag would demand, to thwart armored columns from chewing up German soil and German cities? AWACS mounted no rockets, no cannons; it could not even protect itself except by stealth and maneuver. And why, the Bundestag would challenge, is the Federal Republic paying so much more than the United Kingdom which stands to gain greater economic benefits and at least equal military benefits from AWACS? Then think of the embarrassing questions about why America would not, in return, buy first-rate German equipment like the Leopard II tank or at least its main weapon, the 120 millimeter gun. What price NATO unity?

The British defense establishment regarded prospects for Alliance approval of NATO AWACS in sufficient time a sporting chance at best. The British economy reeled from a succession of blows. The pound sterling was emaciated by spiraling balance-of-payments deficits and persistent double-digit inflation. Energy imports were soaking up capital sorely needed to reindustrialize. And an unhappy and underemployed work force was demanding unaffordable wage settlements. Fold in the seemingly unending loss of blood and treasure in Northern Ireland, the rebellious left wing Laborites, the steady gains by Margaret Thatcher's forces in local elections—and the political picture shone none too brightly either.

Prime Minister Callaghan had already promised to retrench further on defense spending. How much of the proposed cut of £550 million for the next two fiscal years starting 1 April would come from the monies planned for replacing Shackleton Airborne early warning aircraft? And what about the industrial base needed for defense mobilization? What state-of-the-art work would be left for British aerospace industries if Nimrod were terminated? Still, AWACS would be militarily more capable than Nimrod and might even prove less expensive. Key aerospace industries could remain technologically current through collaboration on AWACS production. Then too, the high technology Harrier and Multi-Role Combat Aircraft would keep British industry technologically competitive as well. An English base for NATO AWACS could offer long-term jobs as well as at least incidental, if not nearly full time, surveillance coverage of maritime approaches to the United Kingdom. Certainly, the case could be made for NATO AWACS, but the decision had to be made quickly before more of the money planned for a Shackleton replacement was nibbled away.

The United States' negotiating team brought to Brussels that January a unique variation of the same mixed emotions suffered by the British and Germans. As Department of Defense agents for negotiating the terms of the sale as well as the terms for a share of the buy, they faced pressures from two directions. Allies had already signalled disquietude concerning business arrangements for the sale, and, for that matter, so had Congress.[25] Behind another revetment stood those who would have to fund the buyer's share, the Air Force (from its slice of the defense budget), and Congress.

At first glance, American negotiators seemed to have had little flexibility on the terms of the sale. The contractor's bid represented the bulk of the estimated selling price. To speculate on how much of the bid's profit margin could be negotiated away is one matter; to share that speculation with Allies, who might seize on it as a promised price reduction, quite another. The other large component of the estimated selling price, the cost of equipment and services to be furnished by the Air Force, held no profit margin and hence would appear non-negotiable.[26] Public law dictated the final cost component. Surcharges must be added to the estimated selling price as a means to recover the business costs of arms sales and pro rata portions of prior investments.[27] Babione knew each could be manipulated a bit (as indeed, they eventually were), but he held negotiating instructions reflecting, among other considerations, the Department's worry that Congress might count the "price" of the seller's concessions as part of the buyer's cost share.

Seller's concessions aside, compelling circumstances dictated the limits of the United States' cost share. Dr. Malcolm Currie had in effect etched those limits in stone when he testified to the Congress that an American share of a NATO program would be in the range of 25 to 33 percent.[28] Besides, at some point—the political importance of the NATO AWACS initiative notwithstanding—a too-high cost share may have become self-defeating for economic and military reasons. For a cost share of, say, $750 million, the Air Force could have fielded (and retained control over) another ten of its own AWACS rather than contribute (and relinquish control over) the lesser number of NATO AWACS that same sum would buy.[29] This reasoning, acknowledged by other governments at the time, does not imply that anyone envisaged, much less could have pulled off, such a trade considering the climate in Congress. It simply circumscribes the decision maker's reverence for the logic of using scarce resources in a manner defensible as reasonably cost-effective. Finally, given that competition for resources does not normally permit one weapon system—particularly a controversial one—to consume too much of a single budget request, AWACS' advocates feared a higher share of NATO AWACS' costs would proportionately decrease the already slim prospects for the Air Force AWACS program. These advocates wanted both programs, not one at the expense of the other.

Representatives from several other governments participating in this initial round of financial negotiations signalled similar concerns about the financial burdens posed by the NATO AWACS program. But since the major contributors shared their concerns, they apparently did not feel moved to complain too loudly.

To summarize, reduced cost shares stood as the common goal among governments represented at the first Brussels meeting. Schemes on how best to reach that goal not surprisingly reflected individual government's perceived interests. Thus, a number of European representatives argued alternatively for the United States to pay a higher share or subsidize the sale in some fashion. The Americans, on the other hand, proposed decreasing the level of penalty-laden industrial collaboration in Europe and eliminating or deferring more of the enhanced capabilities several European representatives wanted for NATO's version. These proposals, couched of course in terms more circumspect than presented here, persisted for the nearly two years governments took to negotiate an agreement.

The first meeting of financial experts concluded on the same note that inspired the meeting in the first place. Nations embraced AWACS but not with sufficient ardor to be eager to pay the asking price. Still, problems were now more clearly defined.

Some nations, because of internal budgeting priorities and commitments, wished to delay or reduce the initial increments of their funding shares for two to five years. One immediate remedy was to ask the United States Government to waive any pre-payment of termination liability, which in effect would reduce the amount of money needed in the early years of the acquisition effort.[30] The United States agreed. A second remedy, which took over a year to negotiate, called for those governments with relatively greater financial flexibility to pay the bulk of their respective shares early, thus allowing others with more limited flexibility to pay later. Few suspected both accommodations would in time lead to discomfort and bruised feelings.

Other nations—indeed, all other nations—choked on the cost of doing business with the United States Government. Those surcharges required by the Arms Export Control Act amounted to approximately $125 million for NATO AWACS.[31] Allies knew, however, that same law permitted the Secretary of Defense to waive for AWACS all but about $45 million of the surcharges if such a waiver would promote the standardization of defense equipment in NATO. AWACS qualified hands down. From a European perspective, the cost of doing business also meant tolerating a modest slap at national sovereignty insofar as it can be "tainted" by an American agency's audit of European subcontractors' books.[32] Allies initially noted and in time argued that such business arrangements were totally inappropriate for the unprecedented collaborative effort known as NATO AWACS. It could be too that more than a few Allies, who had long chafed quietly over these indignities, viewed AWACS as a vehicle for change. The American sales campaign was, indeed, a double-edged sword.

Babione resisted stoutly, pointing out that the United States had already swallowed a $440-million forfeiture of pro rata research and development costs (making its effective cost share close to 40 percent), that the Congress would in effect have to sustain additional waivers, and that federal statutes largely prescribed the "onerous" business arrangements. It was proving tough to sell in a buyer's market.

The third and final major problem was not so much identified as it was underscored at the first meeting. Germany's Padberg quietly, but nonetheless adamantly, rejected his government's proposed share. Moreover, he offered scant indication as to what share the Federal Republic might entertain. Like the competent negotiator he proved to be, he contented himself to wait first for a counter proposal from those with greater incentive. Both the American and British negotiators remain persuaded to this day that Padberg held no instructions from Bonn on what might constitute an acceptable cost share for Germany. Leber denies that.[33] In any event, delegates had no choice but to place Germany's position in the "too-hard-to-work-here-and-now" file and agree to a second meeting two weeks hence. The United Kingdom's deadline was fast approaching.

Round One—Second Session

Babione's report initiated a flurry of activity unusual even for the Pentagon. When the dust settled, he had new negotiating instructions, subject as always to congressional ratification:[34]

- The United States would waive asset use and rental charges at a savings to the program of $16 million.
- The United States enjoyed fair confidence that the prime contractor could be persuaded to reduce its bid by $50 million (and, in one of those tragicomic incidents that belie the efficacy of the military-industrial complex, the contractor inadvertently upstaged the government's position by subsequently introducing a best and final bid with a $100 million cost reduction).
- And, *if* such a waiver would make the difference, the United States would forgo, at a $66 million savings to the program, the final 4 percent recoupment of its research and development investment.
- The Department of Defense further promised its help in seeking relaxation of some objectionable business arrangements.

For their part, nations in line to participate in aircraft production agreed to delete, at a savings of $100 million, those industrial collaboration activities with the greatest cost penalties, provided American industry offset the losses with equivalent-value contracts.[35] This concession should not be taken too lightly. Losing many of the deleted items meant losing the potentially long-term competitive advantages stemming from high technology transfers. Germany lost the most—for the moment. The second session never got off the ground. Certainly, Babione never found the opportunity to toss America's game-winning blue chip—total waiver of research and development recoupment—into the pot. Governments had come a far distance in record time, but the question of affordability proved too elusive. Costs in the aggregate had been slimmed considerably through program changes, concessions, and sleight of hand to roughly $2.25 billion. Allocating these costs among nations remained a stumbling block from start to finish.

Why? Because cost exceeded value for one key contributor, the Federal Republic of Germany. This judgment may appear unfair in that it implies a singular culpability where none existed. From a German point of view, the proposed share posed an unacceptable burden. From perhaps a more objective point of view, Germany's share, as specifically proposed in early 1977, posed an unfair political and financial burden. Whatever culpability existed must be shared by the United Kingdom and the United States who, for different reasons, demanded too much too quickly for too little from the Federal Republic at the wrong time. Finally, the statement of cause is unfair because Germany's understandable obstinacy, occupying center stage as it did, masked countless other program issues that could have just as easily delayed the program. Delegates holding dear these other issues apparently saw little point in trying to share the limelight with Germany. Silence, as future events revealed, is not always consent.

2. THE NIMROD DECISION

By the end of the second meeting of national financial experts, Whitehall had surrendered all but the last of any illusions about AWACS. For Britain's Minister of Defence, Mulley, the last illusion would fade a few weeks later in Munich. Germany's unyielding stance, understandable although it may have been in light of the unfair burden proposed, had blocked progress on the issues referred to national experts by ministers. Blelloch, Babione, and LaBerge each had met privately with Padberg during that second meeting, and each had come away with essentially the same answer. For the United Kingdom, the answer meant Nimrod—unless further bilateral approaches to the Federal Republic succeeded in some unexpected way.

A Reluctant Choice

Against the backdrop of two unsuccessful negotiating sessions on cost sharing, Mulley met Leber in February 1977 at the annual Wehrkunde Conference in Munich.[1] The two shared much in common: both served as sergeants during World War II; both began their political careers in trade union movements; both rose steadily in the socialist/labor parties of their countries to become defense ministers; and both were shrewd politicians laboring under trying circumstances. They chatted much of one entire evening about NATO AWACS.

Mulley did not have to elaborate on the predicament he faced. Leber had brought a clutch of clippings from English newspapers detailing (and joining) the ongoing debate over Nimrod and AWACS. Mulley and his Ministry stood almost alone in wanting to give AWACS a chance. To be sure, his cabinet colleagues did little to undermine his preferred choice, but neither would they—or likely could they—agree to cancel Nimrod on the mere hope of a NATO AWACS program. Those British industries who stood to gain from the Ministry's "buying national" suffered no such compunction, and they openly lobbied for Nimrod.

Western defense establishments do not trifle with industrial lobbies any more than the lobbyists trifle with defense establishments. Normally, they do not have to worry the matter, since a confluence of interests make the two groups natural, though wary, allies. In the Nimrod affair, they held opposite views. In the end the lobby's view prevailed—more from circumstances of the moment than from guile or omnipotence.

Not that British industry was content to count on the circumstances alone of a depressed economy and weakened ruling party. The three principal companies involved—Hawker-Siddeley, Marconi-Elliot, and Rolls-Royce—joined forces, with Hawker-Siddeley in the lead, to orchestrate support for Nimrod. They pressured Members of Parliament and the Ministry of Defence. They played to the press, which tilted toward anti-government positions anyway. They also plied their trade union employees with train fare and beer money for a series of telling protests at the House of Commons. They issued fact sheets contrasting the employment opportunities, balance-of-payments considerations, and military capabilities between the British and American system, argued that America wanted to sell AWACS to keep its defense industries viable during the post-Vietnam draw-down, and finally pointed out that the Shackleton replacement program had been initialed long before the NATO AWACS had even been conceived. And they also rushed to display, one week before defense ministers were to meet in extraordinary session, a prototype of the modified Nimrod which, in light of subsequent events, must have been the hollow shell of an airplane.[2] (Displays of such prototypes are standard publicity fare for most nations' aerospace industries.) The timing of this particular display was, of course, designed for public and parliamentary consumption as well. It fed the notion of AWACS someday—maybe—or Nimrod now.

Mulley nonetheless stood prepared to weather the Nimrod storm if he could be assured that NATO would agree on AWACS in the near future. His stand was not altogether unselfish; powerful domestic considerations aside, NATO AWACS could have been defended as the marginally better deal for Britain as measured in military and Alliance political terms. Thus, he looked to Leber for support. But Leber suffered his own set of political problems. Besides, his sense of the political scene in England led him to conclude that Mulley must have just about decided in favor of Nimrod, but was pushing, over German protests, for an early, and therefore unlikely, NATO decision on AWACS so as to legitimatize the Nimrod decision—or at least not to be "blamed" for the failure of NATO AWACS. That honor could go to Germany which, everyone knew, could not or would not yet make a decision on the program.

Given his circumstances—and putting aside any obstacles stemming from the inequity of Germany's proposed share—Leber could not have led his government into the program on the schedule Mulley's circumstances required. Given Schmidt's decree that there could be no budget increase, which among the German military services would step forward to sacrifice defense programs for AWACS? And to forestall Leber's selecting the sacrifices—had he been so inclined—senior German officers let their party and the Bundestag patrons know that AWACS, however important for NATO unity, was not a national military requirement. Leber possessed neither the political clout nor the personal taste to ride roughshod over his generals on this issue.[3] He needed time and a better deal to bring them around.

So it happened in the margins of the Wehrkunde Conference that both Mulley and Leber reasoned the other really did not want AWACS. Mulley needed Leber to pledge a share to AWACS before he could cancel Nimrod.[4] Leber could not. Leber needed Mulley to cancel Nimrod for the political leverage such an action would give Leber in his government. Mulley could not. Each apparently thought the other "would not." And neither knew the other well enough—Mulley having only taken the defense portfolio a few months before—to probe beyond impressions.

Post-Wehrkunde events strengthened Mulley's impression of the impending postponement and perhaps failure of the NATO AWACS initiative. A third meeting of national financial experts was first delayed and finally cancelled. Cost-sharing negotiations had gotten almost nowhere. Governments haggled over scheduling a date for an extraordinary session of defense ministers, promised so readily the preceding December, until the United Kingdom had to insist on a meeting before 1 April. And London (as well as Washington) began hearing rumbles from Bonn about linkages between AWACS and other programs—linkages portending new delays.

The rumbles reflected new realities. Unknown to Mulley or anyone else outside the German Government, Leber had on 3 March 1977 taken NATO AWACS to Germany's Federal Security Council. The Council had agreed to German participation on six conditions:[5] (1) AWACS must be a NATO-wide program; (2) its military value must be proved; (3) financing must be secured both within the Federal Republic and other governments; (4) the German share must fall considerably below America's share; (5) other German defense programs must not be disturbed; and (6) the question of compensation (for Germany's share) must be satisfactorily resolved. Setting aside the apparent contradiction between Schmidt's dictum of no budget increase and the Council's instruction to leave other national defense programs untouched, the last condition alone ensured delay.

His impressions notwithstanding, Mulley placed the AWACS proposition before the Cabinet in March. Despite British industry's lobbying, the deluge of protest letters and rallies to pressure the Commons, and the political and economic climate of the moment, the Cabinet left the choice to him. Mulley had in effect already, albeit reluctantly, decided the question. His defense minister colleagues would, on 25 March, have to change his mind.

Ministers in Extraordinary Session

As he entered Conference Room 16 at NATO Headquarters on the morning of 25 March, Brown might have reasonably suspected Mulley had already decided Nimrod's fate.[6] His private meeting with the British defense minister the evening before ended with Mulley's arguing the merits of a mixed force of Nimrod and AWACS aircraft. It proved to be Minister Mulley's dry run for the ministerials. Luns gavelled the meeting to order shortly after eleven o'clock—the late start necessitated to accommodate the many private bilateral meetings scheduled that morning. It is during these meetings in the margins (as private discussions attendant to plenary sessions are called in diplomatic jargon) that differences are settled, bargains struck, and tactics devised.[7] These meetings often lead directly to the decisions taken in plenary sessions. And such meetings reduce the chances one minister or another might take an unexpected position or voice an unanticipated view. No one likes unpleasant surprises at ministerials.

Luns' welcoming remarks foreshadowed what would emerge as the dominant theme of the day. AWACS would improve NATO's deterrent posture, and, yes, would also signal Alliance solidarity. Not even the Chairman of the Military Committee— Admiral of the Fleet, Sir Peter Hill-Norton—whose official duties and ministerial ritual required him at the outset of meetings to review the military aspects of the question being referred to ministers, dwelt on the military need for AWACS. He too underscored the political meaning of AWACS during his brief remarks. Solidarity, after all, is not an unimportant dimension of deterrence.

Luns next introduced LaBerge to present the proposal, as shaped by financial experts, for the ministers' consideration. His briefing also bordered on the perfunctory, since defense ministers already understood the issues. Their staffs had dissected into digestible pieces the detailed proposal provided to governments the week before. Set on the table in front of each minister or minister's surrogate was his defense staff's contribution to Alliance decision making—an imposing volume of fully-staffed position papers, contingency statements, and background information that only a devotee of detail could appreciate, much less use.

LaBerge saw five key categories of interrelated issues: program costs; national payment schedules; alternatives for France's participation; the status of France and Greece (neither of which was represented at the ministerials); and cost sharing. He had saved the toughest problem for last. Ministers addressed it first and really never moved beyond it.

Mulley opened the discussion and immediately took the offensive. He knew, because Allies share the general outlines of their going-in positions, there would be a move at an appropriate moment to delay the decision in the interest of trying to find some middle ground on cost sharing. He could scarcely agree to that. Thus, Mulley served notice that the United Kingdom could brook no further delay, and unless he could return to London with a signed and sealed agreement on AWACS, the Allies could no longer count on Britain for a cost-share. By his tally, he noted, only about 60 percent of program costs were covered by governments' pledges. That state of affairs hardly promised an early decision.

Canada's Minister of National Defence replied. Although he could not announce Canada's formal decision to participate, Danson stood confidently prepared to seek cabinet approval for any reasonable proposal. But that proposal simply had to include all Allies. Canada, which stood to gain the least evident military benefit from NATO AWACS, appreciated the significance of Alliance cohesion and was willing to pay a share to maintain it.

Brown drove the point home, declaring that the United States had already demonstrated the flexibility sought by the Allies in the name of solidarity. Not only had he agreed to certain cost-reducing waivers, he agreed to increase the American share to 33 percent. With like-minded flexibility on the part of all allied governments, the AWACS initiative would succeed. The question at hand, he observed, loomed larger than the mere acquisition of a military asset.

Germany's Leber spoke at length. The Federal Republic, he reported, said "yes to AWACS." On this he could be certain because he had consulted beforehand with Schmidt, the Federal Security Council, his cabinet colleagues, and relevant committees of the Bundestag. But how, he wondered aloud, could any government agree to a specific share when share levels depended on the number of participating governments? In particular, share levels depended on whether France would participate, and getting France to join the effort would take time—certainly longer than the six days remaining until Mulley's deadline. Leber's argument was slightly specious, but sufficiently reasonable to place Mulley on the defense. Luring France back into a NATO-wide military program, all Allies recognized, would be of such political value that timetables and costs, if neither demanded too much compromise or treasure, might be managed.

Luns continued the poll of governments' views. Belgium's Vanden Boeynants, finding himself in the not unusual position of speaking for a caretaker government, said nothing to derail the proposal or move it along. The Netherlands' newly appointed defense minister, Abraham Stemerdink, perhaps reflecting his countrymen's passion for orderliness and procedure, berated the initiative for not conforming to NATO's (highly imperfect) equipment planning process, but nonetheless tentatively accepted the Dutch share. Turkey's ambassador to NATO, A. Coskun Kirca, accepted a share a bit lower than the one proposed, provided other governments could agree to a forward operating base for AWACS in Turkey. Ambassador Marcel Fischbach, sitting in for Defense Minister Emile Crieps, accepted Luxembourg's proposed share.

As the poll continued, Signor Lattanzio, echoing the remarks he offered fifteen weeks earlier, said that Italy endorsed the need, but could offer little more than moral support and a symbolic contribution of $1 million. (More will be said later about Italy.) Ambassador Anker Svart of Denmark reported that his government would consider participation at a level lower than the one proposed, provided infrastructure funding could be found for Danish coastal defense radars.[8] Portuguese Ambassador de Freitas-Cruz offered a symbolic contribution of $50 thousand plus a fair-share payment for support facilities. Rolf Hansen, who had consented to the chair's request to speak after Canada, had earlier accepted Norway's share subject to manageable conditions.[9] Luns—a skilled tactician aware of uneven support for the program and short on dramatic announcements that might sweep along the reticent—had used the standard parliamentary ploy of calling first on governments holding positive views in an attempt to build what would appear as a ground-swell of support. Norway was a good choice.

In an alliance of independent thinkers that country enjoys a reputation along with a few others of being slightly more independent—possibly because it shares a common border with the Soviet Union. As a flank nation, the direct military benefit of AWACS for Norway's defense was perhaps slightly less evident than for, say, the nations of the central region against whom are massed the bulk of Warsaw Pact forces. As a minor-share nation receiving scant economic benefits from program expenditures, Norway stood to recoup less of its contribution than several others. With respect to this last point, Americans (and other wealthy Allies, but particularly Americans) tend far too often to discount the burden that "only" $20 to $30 million poses for nations like Norway and its four million people and $1 billion defense budget. Allies in the same boat do not discount the burden, thus the relevance of Norway's early supporting remarks.

On balance, the first round of views had not gone too badly. No government disputed the need. All embraced the political symbolism of the program. Several had accepted the cost-sharing arrangements, while the balance had accepted portions of those or countered with lower offers. Except for Mulley, whose ministry had already planned funding for a Shackleton replacement, each speaker added the necessary caveat that his government's participation needed to be ratified through parliamentary processes. Mulley placed himself in a difficult political position when he announced that he could not cancel Nimrod on the basis of assurances, promises, and good intentions. He needed a signed agreement.

Given his circumstances, Mulley probably did need a signed agreement. But to suggest, in effect, that ministers bypass parliamentary processes—which, of course, they could not do—and agree to the program then and there proved to be his undoing. That he had done so in an honest and frank attempt to save Britain's participation in NATO AWACS, if not to save the program itself, moderated the damage not one bit. Luns chewed gently on the proposition. Democratic processes, he noted, generally give parliaments the final say, particularly when the taxpayers' money is involved. And when, he probed, had parliaments approved a program before ministers put the question to them? Mulley retreated. He would accept the risk, he added, of recommending AWACS to his cabinet colleagues if the ministers assembled, subject only to parliamentary approval, would sign on the dotted line that day. Otherwise, he might not be able to hold Britain in the AWACS program. The amendment came too late to prevent a rout.

Leber was the first of a succession of ministers to respond to Mulley's and Lun's exchange. Germany can say "yes" today, he stated, but that "yes" does not apply to two airborne early warning systems ... Nimrod and AWACS. Eighty percent of AWACS costs are pledged by governments here today, he continued, but what incentive would France have to join the program if one hundred percent of the costs were pledged? Norway's Hansen picked up the theme. Two programs do not testify to Alliance solidarity, he noted; how does a divided Alliance negotiate security issues with the Warsaw Pact? Danson of Canada drove the point home by saying he could perhaps take short cuts to secure cabinet approval for AWACS by Mulley's deadline (31 March), but he could promise no success in selling a two-system program. Mulley tried again. "There is a time problem here; you need more time, my government has no more time. Cannot we explore the merits of a compromise," he pled, "wherein my government would proceed with Nimrod now and you would follow with AWACS or whatever when you can?"

Luns wisely cut short what promised to be an acrimonious debate by reminding ministers of the need for an agreed press communique. The unusual session of defense ministers would, he observed, attract unusual interest by the press. For good measure, he called for a temporizing recess. Exchanges went on until eight o'clock in the evening, the last three hours spent in an animated executive session. The final communique captured only a fraction of what had happened:

> The Defence Planning Committee of the North Atlantic Treaty Organisation met in Ministerial Session in Brussels on 25 March 1977, to discuss a cooperative programme to achieve a NATO Airborne Early Warning capability.

Ministers re-affirmed their support for the programme, and decided, subject to approval by competent authorities, that:

> a. An AWACS early warning system will be established;

b. details of nationally suitable cost sharing and some other still open questions will be worked out rapidly;
   c. governments will take all possible steps to establish an agreed cooperative programme by 1 July 1977.

   The United Kingdom Defence Minister, while endorsing fully the importance of the provision of an Airborne Early Warning System for the Alliance as a whole on the basis of collective decision and common funding, reserves the position of his Government as to the best way in which his Government could make its contribution.[10]

Italy's Lattanzio wanted the communique to reflect his government's position as, in indirect fashion, it reflected Britain's all-but-announced Nimrod decision. Luns and other defense ministers wanted to put the best possible face on a failed effort. In the end, Lattanzio conceded that the carefully constructed phrase, "details of nationally suitable cost-sharing," left Italy an out. Clever communique language can mean all things to all people.

The Aftermath

The ministerials had gone badly for Mulley. He was too experienced a politician to have underestimated the sense of theater that occasionally carries ministerial sessions beyond the predictable. He surely knew that ministers, in most instances, have invested decades honing their parliamentary skills— the sense of timing, the sense of how far they can move their governments on a given issue, and the wit to survive by seldom being seen as the direct cause of failure. That defense ministers hold the first or second most important portfolio in their respective governments testifies to their mastery of these skills. Perhaps he had underestimated Leber. Leber had artfully taken Germany off the hook and, with some help from the chair—and a fair measure from Mulley himself—among others, had placed the United Kingdom squarely and securely on the hook. No one seemed to make too much of the fact Italy too had in effect reserved its position, or seemed to care that governments' conditional pledges were, in sum, half a billion dollars short of the amount needed. Yet, because he chose to announce his lack of flexibility to his ministerial colleagues, Mulley became the scapegoat.

Mulley faced up to his bleak choice. First advising his defense minister colleagues by private correspondence a day earlier. Mulley announced to a pleased House of Commons on 31 March 1977 that the United Kingdom would proceed with full-scale development of the Nimrod. His advisory to colleagues, crafted ever so carefully in positive tones, attempted to limit the damage. The United Kingdom, he advised, would unilaterally provide an urgently needed airborne early warning capability for NATO's Atlantic approaches. Nimrod would be, in effect, Britain's in-kind contribution to an Alliance airborne early warning program. And Nimrod, he pledged, would be fully interoperable (able to exchange data) with AWACS or whatever system the Allies might acquire. The advisory served its attempted purpose not a whit—initially.

Reportedly noting that "Nimrod is its own reward," Brown let wither those incentives extended earlier to keep the United Kingdom in the NATO AWACS program.[11] America's planned sample-lot purchase of Hawker-Siddeley's Skyflash air-to-air missile would be cancelled and American-British collaboration on developing a runway penetrator weapon would be delayed. The prospects for a substantial American investment in the advanced Harrier aircraft—already problematic for other reasons and not in any case tied to AWACS—would be eroded further. (The British could not be certain that there was no linkage between Harrier and AWACS.) Apparently fearing a congressional backlash, Britain's ambassador Ramsbotham took the unusual step of communicating Whitehall's side of the AWACS story directly to key leaders in the Congress.[12]

Feelings ran high on the continent as well. Several commentators, for example, spoke openly about "England's defection." Others privately expressed a widely-held conclusion that for political reasons the NATO AWACS main operating base could no longer be located in England.

Irritation—a not infrequent expression of political frustration between strong-willed Allies—subsided as rapidly as it had erupted. Britain, after all, remained a stalwart ally who had stayed the course for a long time against mounting difficulties. Who among Alliance ministers had never bent with the winds of electoral imperatives? Mulley had been as forthcoming as possible under the circumstances. And in a final sweet irony no one anticipated at the time, the Nimrod decision made possible an affirmative NATO AWACS decision. Failure begat consensus, commitment, and silver linings.

Exchanges at that single-topic ministerial session underlined governments' commitment to AWACS as a symbol of NATO's political vitality. In pursuit of success, defense ministers spoke with uncommon candor and acted with an equal measure of courage. Brown had offered to increase the American share to 33 percent and Danson had privately offered to seek cabinet approval for an increased Canadian share if that would spell success. Other ministers discarded their staffs' "wait-and-see" recommendations in favor of extemporaneously supportive statements. Each of these statements would serve as departure points in the next round of negotiations. AWACS' political value inched up a notch.

More important perhaps, the United Kingdom's independent course freed a significant share of high technology economic benefits for redistribution to others. The Federal Republic of Germany, in particular, stood poised to gain some of the benefits demanded by the Federal Security Council. With AWACS' value thus boosted politically and economically, affordability for Germany crept closer to being a moot question.

The Nimrod decision was not without thorns, however. It forced a complete restructuring of NATO AWACS force planning. And the "facts of life" described earlier still affected affordability—exacerbated affordability in fact, given the high fixed costs (and hence higher average unit costs) associated with the acquisition effort. Finally, the Nimrod decision slowed the rush of events. Britain's "no-later-than" deadline had come, been tested, and found inviolate, and now no longer paced AWACS.[13] Discouragement, aimlessness, reflection, and tentativeness, those seemingly universal sequences to disappointing setbacks, consumed the next six months. New beginnings take time.

A Spate of New Proposals

When the United Kingdom dropped out of the program—notwithstanding its pledge of Nimrod as an in-kind payment and other governments' commitments, however uneven, to decide the question by 1 July—NATO AWACS floundered for a time. It was not for lack of effort and ideas.

The NATO staff immediately began drafting a new proposal which would accommodate the reality of Nimrod. Looking to the new schedule—and overlooking (as staffs must) the reasonable conclusion that Nimrod probably invalidated it—they marched at quick step to finish a revised proposal.[14] The new proposal, calling for a mixed force of Britain's eleven Nimrods and eighteen collectively-acquired AWACS, sped to the Military Committee for approval. It would be September, however, before the Military Committee endorsed the revised program. In the meantime, at their regularly scheduled spring meeting some eight weeks after the special meeting on 25 March, ministers reaffirmed the program's importance, but avoided setting new timetables.[15] The 1 July 1977 decision date would come and go without so much as a whimper of protest. Sticky initiatives and summer often tend to be incompatible events in Europe.

Sometime that summer, Germany undertook a quite active role in advocating alternative airborne early warning program initiatives. That each alternative collapsed in due course detracted little from Germany's unexpected advocacy, which some described as a positive turnabout in German thinking toward AWACS. Actually, Germany's advocacy—although unexpected and, what should have been more surprising, curious in its execution—was not inconsistent with events of the preceding six months.

Germany had never rejected AWACS, only the proposed cost-sharing arrangements. The difference, an obvious and important one, may have been obscured during the heat of the finger-pointing exercise attendant to the Nimrod decision. Furthermore, one could understandably mistake the German negotiator's close-to-the-vest negotiating stance as meaning something more substantive. Padberg was of course under tight rein from Bonn, but his limited abilities in English contributed also to others' perceptions that he was stalling. The latter factor played significantly during private meetings in the margins of plenary sessions where others firmed impressions and drew conclusions. Had they stepped back from the rush of events to reflect and reason, and had Germany more readily shared with others its legitimate problems, the AWACS initiative may have succeeded in the spring of 1977.

Germany's first alternative proposal called for the Independent European Planning Group to take the lead in stitching together a revised AWACS program.[16] It was a clever idea. Presenting an AWACS initiative in the Planning Group, established in part to provide a collective buffer against America's preponderant influence in the armaments business, would perhaps at once slow the United States' push for an early decision and invigorate the somnambulant Planning Group. France, belonging to the Planning Group as well, might be more easily enticed into a European-sponsored venture. Italy's defense minister, Lattanzio, chairing the Group at the time, followed through with discussions at senior levels. However, it proved just as difficult to build a consensus without Canada and the United States as with them, perhaps more so in light of their firm support for NATO AWACS and their more than 40 percent aggregate share. The proposal faded away quietly before summer's end. Participants saw little point in publicizing another failed effort.

Germany's next proposal took longer to sink from sight, having excited, for different reasons, both sides of the Atlantic. Leber, seeking some means to enhance the program's value for Germany, proposed that an AWACS' type aircraft be manufactured in Europe. The European airplane could then be fitted with much of the equipment used in the American AWACS. His candidate was the A-300 Airbus manufactured by a consortium that included France and Germany.[17] The concept was politically sound—if one dismissed the minor political damage such a concept would inflict on NATO's drive to standardize weapon systems—but was also economically self-defeating and militarily deficient. Clearly, a change to a European-manufactured airframe would raise the political stakes for success in Europe, particularly in Germany and more particularly (from Leber's view) in France. Airbus sales up to that point had been disappointing. Jobs, national pride, and break-even points do carry political meaning. Unfortunately, costs for re-engineering AWACS avionics into the Airbus would have priced it out of competition.[18] And the A-300, designed to carry heavy passenger loads over medium ranges, came up short militarily as well. Among other deficiencies, it suffered insufficient stamina to compete with AWACS on prolonged surveillance patrols. In the end, even Leber agreed that the Airbus would not work.

Coincident with these two alternative proposals, other senior German officials informally asked their American friends to examine the merits of a two-phase purchase of AWACS.[19] In the first phase, central region nations plus the United States and Canada would, depending on the funds thus available, buy somewhere between ten and fourteen AWACS, presumably for the defense of central Europe. A few years later, the flank nations with a bit of help from Germany, the United States, and perhaps Canada would buy enough to round out the force at eighteen aircraft. Unlike Leber's change in sponsor or change in airframe proposals, the two-phase procurement suggestion quickly gained support in the United States.

It was a siren's song that threatened—however unintentionally—to undo years of work toward achieving a NATO-wide program. Yes, some AWACS would be better than none and an initial buy would at least protect the production line.[20] Some Allies could commit funds earlier than others. Buying defense equipment in affordable increments seemed to make sense and, moreover, followed standard military procurement practices. And, yes, a serious thought from good friends should be taken seriously.

Unfortunately, the arithmetic, the financing, and the politics of the initiative simply would not work. High fixed costs, almost all of which needed to be met very early, amounted to roughly $450 million—this before a single airplane came off the production line.[21] Adding the price of ten to fourteen AWACS to these high fixed costs yielded a sum that, relative to a single, unified program, offered no budget relief at all to the first-phase contributors.

Moreover, buying items in two lots would sacrifice whatever economy-of-scale cost advantages accrued from single lot purchases. And, lead times being what they were (and still are) in aerospace industries, phase two would by force of circumstance follow phase one by such a short time—two or three years at most—as to undercut seriously the stated purpose of the proposal, particularly since the staggered payments schedule in the unified program could accommodate late contributors anyway. Potential political liabilities, once fully weighed, further diminished support for the split-procurement proposal. Many governments moved to support AWACS financially because of the political significance they ascribed to Alliance solidarity. In fact, NATO-wide participation stood as a sine qua non in several capitals. How could a two-phase program pass as an Alliance-wide effort unless the second phase contributors agreed to the notion at the outset? And if they could agree at the outset, why bother with a split procurement?

Despite its deficiencies, the proposal was not finally laid to rest until the Germans themselves disowned it. What it did accomplish in uncertain measures—there seldom being simple cause-effect explanations for such events—was to edge the Pentagon's Office of the Assistant Secretary of Defense for International Security Affairs closer to center stage in the United States' quest for a NATO AWACS program. International Security Affairs, chartered to deal with the policy aspects of political-military affairs, had firmly (and correctly, as it turned out) opposed the two-phase procurement proposal when several other offices in the Pentagon supported it. Partly by coincidence, but more for matching the shift in Washington, much the same thing happened in Germany. Day-to-day negotiating responsibilities for AWACS shifted to the office for political-military affairs in the Central Staff.[22] Whatever the reason—reaction to the split-procurement proposal, coincidence, or cosmic intervention—Germany and the United States joined Canada, first on the mark as usual, in reflecting in their institutional arrangements for program negotiations the notion that NATO AWACS was more a political than a business proposition. The subtle shift in emphasis proved fundamental.

The summer of 1977 also witnessed two other tentative beginnings that in time would profoundly affect the NATO AWACS program. Belgium, never happy with the proposed cost-sharing formulas, circulated a suggestion that proportioned cost shares on the basis of each nation's relative gross domestic product. Its suggestion was a time bomb. The second new idea germinating that summer held greater promise from the beginning. Governments' technical experts began toying with approaches for somehow reducing the costly differences between the American and NATO versions of the AWACS. Both ideas flowered before year's end. While events, tentative beginnings, and changing circumstances danced around them, the NATO staff pressed ahead with pricing the AWACS component of the mixed force proposal. Early estimates placed the cost at somewhat more than $2 billion—a sum promising a by-then familiar refrain from national experts at the next round of negotiations. If governments could not agree to a $2.25 billion program with Britain in for $450 million, how could they possibly share a $2 billion program with Britain out? And why, with a one-third reduction in airplanes, were costs reduced less than 10 percent? The twin bugaboos of high fixed costs and inflation continued to torment the program. Delays cost money.

Undaunted, the Secretary General's office called for a second round of financial negotiations to commence in late September. Loose ends and unknowns mattered less than regaining the political momentum molded by the Nimrod decision.

3. THE SEARCH FOR CONSENSUS

One of the realities in Alliance politics, that NATO and national leaders for obvious reasons care not to acknowledge too openly, is that few major decisions can be taken without the full support of the major partners. This reality, however, fits comfortably within the principle of unanimity, since all partners generally must agree, or at least not disagree, on important courses of action. In seeking unanimity, the major partners, however one chooses to define them, do not often bully their less powerful allies and the less powerful seldom act on the basis of browbeating from their powerful friends. Inducements and accommodation work better.

Such very much was the case for NATO AWACS. The United Kingdom dropped out, in part, because of one major partner's uncertain support. Once Germany announced its support, Britain could no longer tolerate the time it would take to wrap up the far-flung loose ends. The realities for a new proposal stood basically unchanged. Without Germany's full support, the proposal for a mixed force of Nimrod and AWACS would most assuredly fail. With Germany's support, the program still might not succeed unless enough other minor-share governments agreed to participate. In the late summer 1977, the former condition seemed more of a worry than the latter. Despite the number of Germany's suggested alternatives—and, in another sense, because of them—American defense officials did not know where the Federal Republic stood on the program. Leber had said "yes to NATO AWACS" at the March ministerial session, but had intimated on the same occasion that the mixed force might be another proposition. And even though Leber subsequently spoke about picking up the pieces and said nothing at the May ministerial to scuttle the initiative, still other voices in the German government offered less assuring assessments. Then, too, if the mixed-force program were to succeed, Germany would have to accept a level of funding it had previously rejected as unaffordable. The arithmetic would not work otherwise. In short, the time had arrived to discuss the matter privately at fairly senior levels—before the plenary negotiating session in late September.

A Seminal Bilateral

The powerful tolerate being bullied even less than the less powerful. Germany's defense establishment reacted with just the proper touch of coolness to their American counterpart's call for a bilateral exchange of views at the policy level.[1] Brigadier General Wolfgang Altenburg, a deputy for political-military affairs in the Central Staff, would meet on 12 September 1977 with Assistant Secretary of Defense for International Security Affairs, David McGiffert. It was hardly a meeting of counterparts in either a protocol or substantive sense but, allowing for organizational differences, hardly an intolerable snub either. America would pay a price for its sales campaign. But short of adding rudeness to political insouciance, the Germans, having agreed to the meeting, could scarcely afford to show up with nothing constructive to say.

The discussions went well from the start. The exchange of views—once again a diplomatic term with rather elastic meaning, but one sufficiently defined by common usage to exclude any manner of formal negotiation and binding agreement—covered the full range of NATO AWACS issues. Ever so circumspectly, the Germans laid out their observations, propositions, and conditions.

Altenburg, reflecting a position taken on the staffed papers he had brought to the meeting, denounced the two-phase procurement proposal. If Germany ever hopes to secure Bundestag approval for AWACS, we must, he offered, settle on a single number that at least comes close to meeting both the military requirement for Alliance-wide surveillance and the political requirement for Alliance-wide participation. Ten to twelve AWACS would do neither, he argued. Much to the relief of some in the Pentagon, that marked the end of the two-phase procurement scheme (although it did not stop talk of a smaller force). In light of the obstacles remaining to be hurdled, however, it is difficult to say even now which proposal had put the harder test to NATO solidarity.

One minor bomb burst deserved another. Turning to costs, the American delegation outlined its surprise offering. Because of the ongoing explosion in computer technology, a less expensive, higher speed, higher density memory core computer had recently become available that would permit the United States and NATO to build a common airplane meeting most of the enhanced capabilities required by NATO at little or no cost increase to the United States for its national force of AWACS. And, with a few other alterations taken here and there, an eighteen aircraft force of these common AWACS could cost approximately $300 million less than current estimates.[2] The German delegation beamed its approval and promised strong support for the initiative—as much for the cost reduction that promised an affordable program as for a standardized AWACS. That the few other alterations taken here and there accounted for most of the cost avoidance detracted little from the concept of a standardized AWACS. Among Alliance governments, the term "standardization" holds significant political meaning.[3] NATO AWACS' value nudged closer to its cost.

Continuing with cost issues, the American delegation tabled an illustrative cost-sharing scheme excluding France. Altenburg, picking up on the omission, reported that Germany now believed that France, although still interested in AWACS, probably could not commit itself to the program soon enough. Quietly and matter-of-factly stated though it was, Altenburg's comment signalled a fundamental shift in German thinking—or at least a change in what the Germans had been saying. Both sides agreed that the Allies should continue to entice France with AWACS, but no longer would they count on them for a cost share. France, of course, had been saying just that for months. In taking the first steps to remove one major obstacle to program approval, however, another had been simultaneously constructed.

With France out of the calculations, the financial burden for others would mushroom by more than

$200 million. Insufficiently sensitive to the requirement for logical cost-sharing arrangements, which thus would be indefensible before legislatures as equitable, the American's illustrative cost-sharing plan assumed a German share of $650 million and a United States' share of $750 million. These and other shares had been derived more on the basis of judgment than arithmetic. And although the others' shares proved not far off from what governments eventually approved, the United States' judgment of affordability for others could hardly stand up as a compelling argument in national legislatures. The Germans, listening politely, neither accepted nor rejected the cost share and payments schedule. Politeness, as the Americans would be reminded in due course, should never be confused with acquiescence.

Moving closer to the core of Germany's problem with NATO AWACS, the American delegation detailed the industrial benefits potentially available to the Federal Republic in the slimmed-down standardized AWACS program. They amounted to $230 million worth of fairly high technology work.[4] Adding this sum to the economic benefits attendant to hosting the airplane's main operating base, if governments agreed to a German base for AWACS, promised over time nearly to amortize Germany's investment in the program. The Nimrod decision did have its silver linings.

Altenburg seized on the basing question. Under the circumstances, he noted, it would undoubtedly prove most difficult to gain support within the federal government for Germany's large financial contribution to NATO AWACS if the airplane's main operating base was not located in the Federal

Republic. He had understated the case. The German military services viewed AWACS as important, but not so important as to warrant dislocating the equipment modernization programs they had fought hard to win. And a defense budget supplemental request portended its own set of political risks for the Social Democrats, even if Chancellor Schmidt may have changed his mind on the question. Consequently, it would take more than political maneuvering to carve out from planned spending levels enough deutsche marks to pay for AWACS. McGiffert pledged America's support if a German base would assure a NATO-wide AWACS program and if NATO's military authorities could endorse locating the main operating base in Germany. Affordability for Germany strode into view.

Moreover, Altenburg casually continued, there were some in the government who strongly believed that America's decision on the heavy caliber gun for its new main battle tank should be linked to Germany's decision on NATO AWACS.[5] McGiffert said nothing and Altenburg, too much a gentleman and soldier-statesman to press, dropped the subject. On 31 January 1978, the Department of Defense announced that the United States Army had selected the German-designed 120 millimeter smooth-bore gun for its new XM-1 tank. Absolutely no evidence exists to suggest a political linkage dominated American thinking and plenty of test data and analyses do exist to defend on merit alone the Army's selection. Elements of the United States Army and the Congress apparently thought otherwise.[6]

At the conclusion of the meeting, the German delegation raised, and the Americans parried, a number of additional points already identified as potentially threatening issues—business arrangements for the sale, frequency allocations for AWACS in Europe's crowded electronic environment, and others—for which the day of reckoning could be slipped until the more rudimentary questions had tentative answers. Those would be posed, and perhaps partially answered, during the early stages of the second round of negotiations. Later would be soon enough for second order questions.

An Honest Broker

However, even the initial call for a second round of negotiations required some negotiation. Not all capitals thought sufficient detail on the mixed-force proposal would be available for review by national experts in late September. The Federal Republic of Germany, in particular, resisted an early meeting on the logical premise that negotiations among senior representatives—that is, at Padberg's level—could not be productive until substantive choices could be placed before them. The initial session would not likely offer such choices. In the end, partly as a result of the promise stemming from the American-German bilateral discussions but mainly through the good offices of NATO's senior staff, Germany agreed to send a representative at an appropriate level. The staff simply pointed out that all other governments except France and Iceland would be represented. A modest and obvious tactic, of course, but the simple and commonplace should never be confused with the unimportant. One of the more significant features of Alliance decision making had just been demonstrated.

Few observers would articulate the need in the same terms, and many may deny the need even exists, but certain kinds of NATO initiatives do require the services of an honest broker—a relatively objective multinational staff body that can mediate the understandably narrower interests of coalition partners. The slightly contentious question of mediation aside, all recognize the need for a supporting staff in NATO that can attend to capturing on paper the statements, propositions, and factual details necessary for decision making. Indeed, the need is formally incorporated into NATO's staff structure: the International Military Staff serves the Military Committee; the International Staff supports the Office of the Secretary General. Both staffs do provide a mediation function—insofar as a clearing house can provide a kind of mediation for principles—and both staffs did, of course, work important aspects of the NATO AWACS program. However, the great bulk of staff support for NATO AWACS came from the NATO Airborne Early Warning Programme Office, provisionally established under the auspices of the North Atlantic Council to support on a daily basis the Assistant Secretary General for Defence Support.[7] Of the Programme Office's manifold contributions to NATO AWACS, serving as an honest broker may have been the most important and least noted.

Germany's change of heart on the initial call for a second round of negotiations stands as one very minor example of an honest broker's role. Important examples preceded that one—dividing major-share and minor-share governments into two groups for cost-share allocation purposes comes immediately to mind—and even more important instances would follow throughout the second round of negotiations and beyond.

The Programme Office profoundly affected the program in another, totally unintended fashion. In 1976, the American, British, and German defense establishments each contributed funds to operate the office and cover the costs of contract definition activities.[8] Principally as a result of those contributions, both the American and German legislatures, in effect, forbade further contributions until the NATO AWACS program became a reality. Although the Department of Defense notified the Congress beforehand of its intention to contribute a share of preparatory costs from reprogrammed Air Force AWACS monies, the Congress, in authorizing seed money for NATO AWACS the next year, restricted the further obligation or expenditure of the funds "until at least one member country of the North Atlantic Treaty Organization (other than the United States) enters into a contract to purchase the AWACS aircraft."[9] The restriction's root meaning was quite clear. The Congress simply would not abide the use by the Department of Defense of taxpayers' money to prefinance the sale of AWACS. In retrospect, the limitation caused no great harm, although it did, as will be seen, lead directly to a lot of anxious moments in the Pentagon. The same could be said of the restriction placed on German money by the Bundestag.

Round Two—First Session

National financial experts reassembled in Brussels on 29 September 1978 for what had been billed as an exchange of information and views. There would perhaps be an opportunity to preview other governments' preliminary negotiating posture as well, but their mildly querulous reaction to the earlier call for negotiations—when little new information on the restructured program seemed available—had persuaded the NATO staff to settle for a less substantive session. The Programme Office, clinging to an ambitious schedule, still hoped to place the matter before ministers for a decision in December. It would take five plenary negotiating sessions, innumerable bilaterals, and a heart-stopping, last-minute flurry to secure the program some fifteen months later. Forging unanimity requires patience. Of the changes in governments' representatives from the first round eight months earlier, two stood out as particularly significant:

- Germany's Colonel Schmidt-Petri, then assigned to the Military Politics and Command Staff in the Federal Ministry's Central Staff, was an amiable career Army officer who shared General Altenburg's vision of AWACS' political and military significance and who was, therefore, willing to take chances.

- United States Air Force Major General Richard C. Bowman, Director of European and NATO Affairs in the Office of International Security Affairs—an incurable Atlanticist more appreciated in Europe than at home, who combined imagination, daring, and persistence—represented the United States.

LaBerge's successor, John B. Walsh, chaired the session.[10] As it turned out, prior concerns in capitals about the meeting's lack of substance proved unwarranted for reasons that could not have been anticipated. Foundations for much of the program's final form were either marked out or poured at this first session.

The Programme Office offered the first imaginative notion. In briefing representatives on the program's status—a customary first order of business in NATO and elsewhere—the Programme Office calculated the value of Britain's in-kind contribution of eleven Nimrod aircraft at $600 million, a sum approximately equal to the cost of the nine forgone AWACS. By then assigning the United Kingdom a percentage share based on the estimated cost of the composite program, all others' shrank proportionally. This computation, although arguably a more accurate reflection of the governments' relative financial burdens, did not impress those representatives worried more about finding absolute sums in already beleaguered budgets than defending those sums before parliaments as relatively more equitable. Nor did it particularly impress John Barry, Blelloch's replacement, who expressed sympathy for the reasoning behind the computation while gently rejecting it.

Unlike many Allies, the United Kingdom does not publicize the cost of its defense programs in the press, or, for that matter, to its friends. But the composite cost notion did offer utility to the American and, in a different way, German defense establishments. For the United States, percentage had mattered slightly more than absolute cost ever since Currie's "25 to 33 percent" statement before Congress two years earlier. For the Federal Republic both percentage and absolute cost mattered a lot, but earlier that year it had argued more against its share relative to Britain's and America's than it had against the actual sum being sought. That argument weakened now that the United Kingdom and Germany owned roughly equal shares. The American-German percentage spread wanted by the Security Council remained largely unaffected by Nimrod's cost.

With or without Britain's $600 million, Belgium objected to the proposed cost-sharing arrangements because they were dated by two decades of economic and political change. Belgium insisted—and, with Walsh's farsighted help, would persuade a majority to agree by the next meeting—that the Programme Office use current economic indices rather than traditional formulas to compute cost shares. It took others to appreciate the paradox of Belgium insisting on a new cost-sharing arrangement while being unable to commit to its proposed aircraft acquisition share.

Bowman served the next offerings. In fairly rapid succession, he outlined the standardized AWACS proposal and discounted the near-term prospects for French participation in the program while concomitantly asserting that eighteen standard AWACS were nevertheless affordable. He argued circumspectly—as he must since other governments had also offered candidate airfields—for locating the main operating base in Germany. Finally, he signalled America's willingness to reconsider special business arrangements for the sale. Negotiations with Allies, from Bowman's point of view, normally should aim for optimal military and political results as long as the business and economic arrangements remain tolerable. There were more than enough others—on both sides of the Atlantic—holding the opposite view to balance any possible excesses. Unarguably, however, Bowman's approach at this particular session did at least reinvigorate the AWACS initiative. Delegates had plenty of substance to digest.

Most reacted favorably to the standard AWACS proposal. The Programme Office's Manager, Air Commodore David M. Scrimgeour, noted approvingly that the American initiative complemented technical experts' ongoing efforts to reduce costly differences between the NATO and Air Force AWACS.[11] Scrimgeour's support immediately added another measure of legitimacy to the proposal, perhaps a double measure in light of his reputation for evenhandedness and his "third-party" status as a British officer managing an effort in which his government would no longer substantively participate. Walsh sustained momentum by offering to ask NATO's military authorities to comment formally on the standardized machine's value. Financial experts properly deferred on the military and technical merits of a standard AWACS while warming to the affordability it promised.

Several representatives, however, resisted the notion of dropping France from the cost-sharing calculations, although everyone agreed that the uncertainty of its participation needed to be resolved urgently. That the specter of French participation continued to haunt the program long after that country had formally demurred remains somewhat of a mystery. Formal demurral notwithstanding, mixed signals from France contributed to the uncertainty. France had, without coaxing, contributed $100 thousand for NATO's preliminary studies on airborne early warning systems, and was known to be quite interested in establishing a commercial base for its premier engine contractor's new jet engine by having it used on the NATO AWACS. France had informally asked for cost estimates on subscribing to the program.[12] On the other hand, the French Air

Force openly opposed NATO AWACS, and conventional wisdom suggested that those of Gaullist sentiment would, on political grounds, resist joining a NATO-wide military program. The balance of the Alliance skirted the question many months later by agreeing that a French share, should it happen, would be used to reduce pledged shares, not buy airplanes.

The Dutch and Portuguese delegates, whose governments had also offered the airfields to serve as the AWACS' main operating base when the more obvious choice of an English base dropped by the wayside, not surprisingly disagreed with Bowman's assertions on base location. Both governments must have sensed the inevitable answer to the question, however, because neither ever chose to exercise NATO's version of a veto by placing a reservation on the consensus decision to locate the base in Germany.

Locating military forces in NATO tends at times to be a tricky matter. Political leaders all agree military imperatives should dictate the answers, yet all keep an eye on political requirements and economic considerations as well, particularly when the choice is not clear-cut militarily, such as was the case with NATO AWACS. To their credit, political leaders do not pressure military authorities to stand firm on one of several fuzzy choices. Thus, with respect to a main operating base, Alliance military authorities used military operations criteria to narrow the choices and properly left the political decision on the narrowed choices to the Council. Defense ministers in due course accepted the German base.

Discussions on business arrangements, using the term's broadest meaning, consumed more time than any other topic. Logically, one would suppose that such discussions would follow a decision to buy the airplanes but, in this program, business arrangements played a signal role in shaping the decision. Obtaining exceptions to America's normally rigid approach to arms sales would have political meaning in capitals, and these would also reduce costs which, in turn, would affect affordability in its other dimension. Virtually all of what the delegates discussed, however tentative and vague, during that first session eventually found its way—along with even more far-reaching terms and conditions—into the decision document placed before ministers for approval. The United States would waive asset use and rental charges. The Department of Defense would serve as NATO's agent in contracting with American suppliers and manufacturers, thereby eliminating the bulk of surcharges for program administration. The Department of Defense would also reconsider the Allies' plea to waive all research and development surcharges, and would seek waiver of the requirement for non-American vendors to use American procurement and accounting standards. The politicization of business arrangements, some would discover later, cut two ways.

Financial experts closed the first session by agreeing to meet in a month's time. The meeting had included considerably more than an exchange of views and information, but considerably less than negotiation on the stickiest issue, cost-sharing. Help would come from unexpected quarters in perhaps an unintended way.

Second Session—The Belgian Proposal

The Belgian cost-sharing proposal completely dominated the second meeting of national financial experts. One early victim was the plan to wrap up a proposal defense ministers could at least review at their December meeting. Belgium's silence, when others occupied center stage, did not mean consent.

Belgium stood on solid ground in arguing that NATO's current burden-sharing formulas—from which NATO AWACS' cost shares would be largely derived—did not reflect ability to pay. Consider, for example, that Germany pays somewhat less than five times more than Belgium for commonly funded infrastructure projects, yet enjoys a gross domestic product nearly seven times as great. Or that the Netherlands, with a gross domestic product 30 percent greater than Belgium's, pays a lesser infrastructure budget share.

Belgium's argument started to come apart, however, when one considered the complete picture on which equitable burden sharing must be based. Germany, for example, at the time paid a higher percentage of its national product for the common defense than did Belgium—3.4 percent for Germany to 3.1 percent for Belgium. The United States unilaterally provides virtually the whole of a strategic nuclear umbrella for NATO and, along with Canada, pays for the defense of that often-overlooked part of NATO territory known as northern North America. Canada, which pays more than Belgium for commonly funded infrastructure projects, receives almost no economic benefits for its contribution while Belgium receives considerable benefit. Then there are whole sets of blurry imponderables to consider. What value, as opposed to cost, should be ascribed to the large standing forces maintained, for example, by Greece and Turkey? At what level of increased defense spending would the anti-defense minority in certain countries gain enough temporary converts to topple pro-defense governments? It is little wonder that those charged with negotiating NATO infrastructure budget shares every five years depart in tiny increments from long-established, and thus politically safer, burden-sharing arrangements.

Still, Belgium's proposal enjoyed support from the majority—probably because it reduced cost shares for ten governments, although not all of the ten sided with Belgium. NATO AWACS would be unprecedented in more ways than one.

Belgium's specific proposal appears more complicated than it actually was. Using statistics compiled by the Organization for Economic Cooperation and Development and NATO's International Staff, the Belgian delegation computed a gross domestic product per capita value for each nation, reduced that amount by $500 per capita to account for those living at subsistence levels, and then multiplied the result by population to arrive at an adjusted gross domestic product.[13] They next divided each nation's adjusted product into the sum of all participating nations' adjusted product to arrive at a percentage figure. Finally, they halved the percentage figure for minor-share governments (to compensate, as did LaBerge's compromise formula, for the fact they would receive no important economic benefits from program expenditures) and proportionally increased the major contributors' percentage shares to reach a 100 percent total. The American share, not surprisingly, skyrocketed to over 60 percent.

Many of the delegations whose governments' cost share stood to be reduced by Belgium's widely supported proposal expressed sympathy for America's plight. More important, all recognized the United States could never agree to such a share, particularly on top of waiving nearly $500 million worth of normally chargeable expenses. Indeed, the United States could unilaterally acquire close to eighteen of its own AWACS for the same sum. The AWACS initiative could have collapsed then and there and most likely much earlier if the Allies—as many observers theorized at the time—really did not want the program. That the initiative did not collapse clearly demonstrated the Allies wanted AWACS, but on affordable terms.

Delegates rejected variations on the Belgian theme almost as fast as others proposed them. Scrimgeour offered a Programme Office variation. Minor-share governments would pay three-quarter rather than half shares and the United States would receive full pro rata recoupment of its investment in research and development, thereby reducing America's net share to about 40 percent. Germany's Schmidt-Petri offered a most subjective variation. The Federal Republic would voluntarily increase its share to 25 percent and other European governments might consider increasing theirs proportionally as well. John Anderson of Canada suggested total defense expenditures be factored into the equation. Bowman suggested that the three major procurement partners fund, say, 80 percent of aircraft costs.

The Dutch representative then offered a piggyback variation of the American variation, wherein fewer aircraft would be procured. That caught the attention of flank nation representatives who intimated that, since force reductions would probably result in fewer surveillance missions on the flanks, their governments' support hinged on a full force being acquired.

Walsh finally changed the subject by noting—wryly, one supposes—that all of the variations yielded results within 10 percent of each other and that was close enough for him to prepare a new proposal for governments' consideration. Buying time, as Walsh well understood, sometimes serves a purpose.

Representatives discussed other issues as well—payment schedules, business arrangements, basing locations—but there seemed little point in getting too excited over what then stood as second-order questions. Financial experts would reconvene in one month. Defense ministers could spend their time in December on subjects other than AWACS.

Sessions Three and Four

Creativity springs from keen senses and open minds. Listening carefully helps, too. Colonel Robert Eaglet, Scrimgeour's American deputy, had developed a creative version of the Belgian cost-sharing proposal by combining portions of the variations suggested over the preceding year and adding a few twists of his own.

After consulting with Walsh and Scrimgeour, Eaglet proposed a "fresh start" cost-sharing arrangement. He retained Belgium's scheme with a couple of important exceptions. First, he set aside "controversial" costs (cost penalties for industrial collaboration, which minor-share nations should not have been expected to bear anyway, and the 4 percent surcharge for research and development), then computed minor shares using the Belgian construction. He next subtracted the sum of minor shares from total aircraft acquisition costs, folded back in the controversial costs, and assigned the resultant total to the three major-share nations. Lastly, Eaglet invited Canada, Germany, and the United States to divide this aggregate in some mutually acceptable fashion taking into account economic benefits and prior investments in research and development. Program administration costs—the second of four major cost components in the program—would be allocated among governments on the basis of the politically acceptable civil budget formula.[14] The costs of support facilities (bases and ground environment modifications—the third and fourth major cost components) would be shared on the basis of the most recently approved infrastructure budget formula. The United Kingdom, having already agreed to do so, would pay a fair share of ground environment modification costs since Mulley had pledged Nimrod's interoperability with AWACS and, by extension, NATO's air defense ground environment.

Eaglet's variation worked! Not all delegates at the 21 November session could promise their respective government's financial support for acquisition shares, but neither did anyone reject the "fresh start" formula. New and more formal estimates of a standard AWACS program lent additional moment to the proceedings as well. Non-aircraft components of the program had increased in cost, but savings from standard AWACS were sufficiently great to reduce total program costs to about $1.9 billion. Part of the cost reduction resulted from the Shah's order for seven Iranian AWACS.[15]

Italy's representative, of course, stuck to his government's offer of a $1 million symbolic contribution. Otherwise he might have formally objected to any formula calling for Italy to carry a $100 million share with no economic return of consequence. Over the next few months the Italian delegation pressed for others to accept the symbolic contribution as Italy's best and final offer, which was refused. Moreover, the others refused even to consider picking up the balance of Italy's share or to meet the costs of modifying the air defense ground stations in Italy, save the one needed to keep Italian sites in the common grid and thus close an otherwise uncovered opening in NATO's air defense perimeter. The refusal was part real and part tactical.

Some capitals really did have a political requirement for the program to be Alliance-wide. And while they sympathized deeply with—and, in fact, had moved to help alleviate—Italy's dire economic problems, they also believed those problems sufficiently transient to permit Italy at least to consider some greater share in the future. Tactically, a united front against Italy's stand would not go unnoticed in Rome. Unless an issue involves deep-seated principles, few allies choose to ignore the plea of all others. Conversely, unless the stakes are extraordinarily high, few choose to press an issue with another ally on a course of action when that objection is based on principle. Italy had all but invited a common assault on its position when it announced that severe economic problems, not principle, dictated the symbolic contribution it was asking others to accept. As a sovereign state, Italy obviously did not need permission or approval from its allies to contribute a symbolic sum toward NATO AWACS. Italy, however, cares very much about its membership in the North Atlantic Alliance, and, as will be seen presently, this feeling, when mixed with the proper catalyst, led Italy to a change of heart.

In the margins of the third session, the American, Canadian, and German delegations met informally to discuss division of the aggregate share of aircraft costs allocated to them. This amounted to about $1,375 million, or about 85 percent of the total. By adding in the costs of Nimrod (by then reduced to $500 million) and accounting for shares of non-aircraft costs—another $185 million for the three—the United States could accept a total share of some $800 million without exceeding the 33 percent limit set, in effect, by the Congress. Without excessive ado but with the clear understanding no commitments had been undertaken, Germany accepted a $590 million share and Canada a $175 million share.[16] All agreed any reduction in industrial collaboration penalties would be credited dollar for dollar to the share of the nation whose industry was involved.

Perhaps basking in the afterglow of a breakthrough on cost sharing—a year in the coming—the German representatives may have exceeded their instructions from Bonn. Earlier and subsequent events certainly suggest that was the case. Perhaps, though, Schmidt-Petri had heeded Anderson's injunction to representatives that there could be no progress if delegates simply parroted known national positions. Ministers had charged financial experts to negotiate an agreement. Negotiations among allies, to succeed, require openness of mind, a confident sense of perspective, and a dash of courage.

Having achieved broad, if not quite unanimous, support for its acquisition cost-sharing proposal, the Programme Office with Walsh at the helm turned to the next contentious issue: proportioning among governments the AWACS' operations and support costs, roughly $100 million annually. The minor-share governments, with Belgium on the point, understandably argued that the same proportions used for investment costs should, for about the same reasons, apply to recurring costs. Just as fervently, Canada, Germany, and the United States, collective victims of such an arrangement, argued the merits of using the traditional formula for sharing the costs of commonly funded military operations: NATO's military budget.[17] Canada offered a particularly cogent argument.

His government, Anderson observed, could justify a higher acquisition share because it stood to gain short-term industrial benefits commensurate with the higher share. No such justification existed for a higher Canadian share of recurring costs. Indeed, it would receive no practical economic benefits from those. Germany and the United States also held firm—even though neither could use Canada's argument—as much for tactical advantage as for any other reason. An obvious compromise, wherein the difference would be halved except for a few case-by-case adjustments, stood waiting in the wings. To move forward too soon could jeopardize the compromise. The Netherlands moved first, followed by Norway and then Denmark, to support a compromise—despite the increased cost that a compromise meant for each. Before the end of the fourth session on 10 January 1978, no government flatly rejected the compromise, even though a few withheld endorsement. On occasion, a "maybe" has to suffice.

78   THE SEARCH FOR CONSENSUS

National experts had at last hammered out a financial framework for a program—soft in too many respects, tenuous in others, but a framework nevertheless. They agreed to meet for a final session in early February to confirm tentative agreements and attack the remaining issues. Of the many remaining issues, two promised particular difficulty: Italy's unpledged share; and payment schedules for nations. The latter, an innocent-appearing issue, masked a profound divergence of views that would linger long after defense ministers approved the program.

Round Two—A Final Session

Spirits were high as delegates filed into Conference Room 10 at NATO Headquarters on 9 February 1978.[18] A month had passed since the last plenary negotiating session, but the honest broker had kept capitals astir with informal reports of progress in other places. Someone from somewhere had reliably reported, accompanied by the standard dictum "please protect" (the source), that Italy might find a way to move beyond a symbolic contribution. The American and German delegations—the latter now headed by Padberg because substantive choices were at hand—held less reason for joy. Two days earlier, they had met privately in Bonn to discuss cost shares, payments schedules, and all that both included and portended. Over lunch they discussed in passing Leber's resignation. A brace of months would pass, however, before that event touched NATO AWACS.

The more immediate problem was Germany's proposed cost share in its several interrelated dimensions: amount, phasing, and anticipated return.

Padberg shared with Bowman the Federal Ministry's tentative thinking on each. The sum of them, of course, circumscribed Germany's view of affordability.

The amount remained too high. Germany had in mind a $550 million or 30 percent share. At the same time, Padberg apparently recognized that Canada and the United States suffered insufficient flexibility to pick up the difference even if the Germans could muster a cogent argument for a shift in shares. Other self-evident approaches spared them the effort. One could reduce program costs, reduce cost penalties for Germany's industrial participation, or increase Germany's economic benefits to reach the same end. And, whatever the approach or combination of approaches, cost growth could be precluded if the United States would guarantee the price. The Americans could not do much about the last, overarching requirement—there being a law to contrary purposes—except to extend unsatisfactory reassurances.[19] But the Americans, Germans, and providential circumstances could and did in due course do something about the first three approaches.

In preparation for the bilateral, Padberg and his staff had also searched out those projects and activities in the German defense budget where excisions for AWACS would cause the least hemorrhaging. By stretching, deferring, or otherwise changing twenty separate programs, Padberg had located enough funds to cover a $550 million-plus share.[20] Unfortunately, the bulk of the money would not be available until 1982 and beyond, when Germany enjoyed more budget flexibility. The United States and others would have to cover most costs until then. And dislocating twenty national programs also meant having to contend with twenty irate advocates and a greater or lesser number of political patrons holding forth in Bundestag committees. The risks were mounting. Finally, Padberg insisted—and the Americans, of course, readily agreed—that Germany should not be penalized for paying most of its share later in the program. Unhappily, each side knew even then that "penalty" meant something different to the other.

Neither side would have quarreled, however, with the notion that economic benefits favorably affect the value factor in an affordability equation. These can be argued more convincingly—or at least compared with economic costs on the same scale more easily—than political or military benefits. Consequently, it was small wonder German defenders of NATO AWACS viewed economic benefits as the one irrefutable argument against those in the Federal Ministry who railed at the cutting of their program to accommodate AWACS, or against those in the parliament or elsewhere who discounted its political and military benefits. And, of course, "compensation" remained a Security Council condition for German participation. As resistance stiffened, the need expanded for heftier counter arguments.

Sadly, and perhaps unfairly, other events in another context from a different time conspired against the Federal Ministry's openly using benefits from the AWACS' main operating base as a principal economic argument to counter its detractors in the Federal Republic. Germany still chafed over having paid to offset, partially, the balance-of-payments debit incurred by America from maintaining a large military presence on German soil. By hard-won agreement in late 1976, Germany terminated the payments begun nearly a decade earlier when bilateral relations reflected different political and economic circumstances. Not only would Germany understandably balk at resuming offset payments, it similarly balked at even acknowledging that hosting military forces yielded any economic benefits. The Germans argued, and one is hard pressed to disagree, that deployment of military forces in NATO must be based on military imperatives, not on economic, political, (or social) considerations.

The Federal Republic was unarguably correct in principle, but perhaps wrong in applying that to NATO AWACS. Unlike the clear military need to station military forces along the Central Front, these aircraft—from a purely military standpoint—really did not have to be stationed in Germany. However, military factors can seldom be divorced from Alliance political considerations in peacetime (and history suggests the same may well hold true in wartime). That being the case, the economic benefits from locating the base in Germany should have been counted. They never were.

With basing benefits thus discounted—rightly or wrongly—the Federal Ministry looked for economic benefits elsewhere. Increasing industrial collaboration on AWACS would be self-defeating because cost penalties would negate, if not exceed, economic benefits. Thus, benefits and counter arguments would have to come from procurement initiatives other than AWACS.

Against this (unseen) backdrop of the American-German bilateral, national financial experts turned to the two known issues blocking a negotiated recommendation to governments. Walsh and the Programme Office finessed the issue of Italy's symbolic aircraft: eighteen standard AWACS if Italy agreed to a full share or if France subscribed to the program; sixteen standard AWACS if both Italy and France maintained their positions.

Reactions varied. Many delegations used the occasion to pressure Italy one more time by asserting that their parliaments might not accept the cost-sharing arrangements without an equitable contribution from Italy. The Programme Office seemed inclined to take Italy's position at face value and, therefore, leaned toward submitting a single proposal for sixteen aircraft. The Americans opposed any proposal making it easier for Italy to stay out of the program. Bowman's stand, which may have appeared insensitive in light of Italy's well-documented economic problems, was founded on inside information. Italy's new defense minister, Atilio Ruffini, and new armaments director, General Fabio Moizo, might succeed in generating cabinet support for a fuller share. They had recently agreed to try at America's request, but they needed time. And they certainly did not need the political and personal grief of having their efforts undermined by a proposal that explicitly excluded Italy. Ruffini and Moizo needed to be able to argue that other allies counted on Italy not to break ranks on NATO's solidarity.

By agreeing to submit parallel proposals to defense ministers, however, financial experts opened the floodgates for a device used sparingly up to that point for coping with uncertainties. From then on, those delegates holding divergent thoughts or, more typically, different instructions could reserve on the consensus view by simply adding a disclaimer. And they did. As footnoting advanced, the incentive for negotiating a unanimous recommendation to ministers receded. More important, the viability of a document adequate for implementing a multinational, multibillion dollar program weakened. Footnotes perpetuated uncertainty.

Still, the advent of the dissenting footnote speeded negotiations. The issue of national payments schedules, for example, proved remarkably easy to negotiate via the footnote. Consider first the nature of the problem. Representatives had agreed a year before to allow those governments with fully committed defense budgets to defer payments until sometime later in the seven-year acquisition effort. As it happened, all but five of the thirteen participating governments reported a need to defer some portion or all of their annual payments for periods ranging up to five years. Unfortunately, the sum of annual payments thus available was insufficient to cover program funding requirements in the early years of acquisition. These funding requirements, constructed to reflect a reasonably efficient production schedule, could be slipped only if nations would accept the cost penalties driven by production inefficiencies and additional years of compounded inflation. The Programme Office, ever an honest broker, suggested a compromise.

Eaglet proposed that all governments accelerate their payments proportionally to a point where annual contributions matched annual funding needs. The governments reporting a need to defer payments objected that their defense budgets really held no slack for such a compromise. Others argued that the compromise penalized those governments who had obligingly agreed to pay from the outset of the acquisition effort. But if one accepts at face value—as one must—governments' declared needs for deferred payments, then all were penalized proportionally, at least in political terms. Such was the stuff of compromise even if the results yielded awkward financial arrangements that the succeeding generation of program managers would decry. And if the footnoted reservations placed by three late-paying nations undermined the compromise agreement, as they most certainly did, then they seemed at the time a small price to pay for concluding a year of fitful negotiations.[21] Further delay would cost money which, in turn, could jeopardize the hard-won agreement. An imperfect document then held a much greater chance of success than a perfect document later.

With plenary session negotiations concluded, Walsh and the Programme Office turned to the task of capturing the results in a document for governments' review. No sooner had this been passed to NATO's Council in permanent session than it needed amendment. The first amendment detailed a reduction of nearly $70 million in estimated acquisition costs.[22] The second transmitted to capitals a copy of a letter to Luns from Italy's defense minister. Ruffini's letter set out the terms and conditions of Italy's full, but qualified, participation in the program. Governments greeted both amendments with enthusiasm.

The Italian Amendment

Italy's military services, not unlike many others in Europe, viewed AWACS as less a breakthrough in air battle management than a potential usurper of national defense funds.[23] Not only would the service chiefs do nothing to support the program, they quietly campaigned against it on the grounds that it served a limited military purpose. Support would have to come from senior political levels in the Ministry of Defense.

Minister of Defense Vito Lattanzio had traveled to Brussels in March 1977 prepared to announce Italy's nonparticipation to his colleagues meeting in extraordinary session. Sometime during the course of discussions that afternoon, he changed his mind. The Allies' declared political need for unity on AWACS moved Lattanzio, an ardent advocate of NATO, to offer a $1 million symbolic contribution. Although much misunderstood, the contribution represented exactly what he advertised it to be, a token payment intended solely to preserve the Alliance-wide character of the program. However meager the amount may have seemed, any contribution from Italy under the circumstances entailed political risk for Lattanzio. He extended the offer without prior consultations with his cabinet colleagues and without support from Italy's military establishment. In so doing he could have invited the kind of charges that led to his predecessor's downfall.

In March 1979, a constitutional court convicted and jailed former Minister of Defense Mario Tenassi for accepting under-the-table payments from agents of Lockheed Corporation to promote the sale of C-130 aircraft in Italy.[24] The conviction followed more than two years of rumors and gossip, leaks to the press, parliamentary investigations and recommendations, and consideration of the charges by the high courts of Italy. In the immediate aftermath of suspicion and cynicism engendered by initial rumors of the Lockheed scandal, Lattanzio dared not overrule his military service chiefs, particularly for an expensive and controversial airplane manufactured in America. It apparently mattered little to Lattanzio that the Alliance-wide character of the program would seem to have placed him above suspicion. However, Italy's Christian Democrats, in danger according to public opinion polls of losing a general election scheduled for mid-1977 to the Communist Party of Italy, could not then afford the slightest hint of impropriety. Post-election circumstances were not much better. The Christian Democrats' narrow victory left little room for maneuvering to keep Italy's Communist deputies from holding government portfolios.

The prospects for Italian participation changed when Ruffini replaced Lattanzio during one of Italy's frequent cabinet shuffles. Some reasons for this were relatively obvious. The Christian Democrats had managed to form a coalition government without the "historic compromise." Time and succession had dulled the initial impact of the Lockheed scandal. The AWACS initiative had by then edged much closer to realization. Other governments had rejected Italy's symbolic contribution for AWACS. And Ruffini, of course, brought his own experiences, values, and ambitions to office. Other reasons were not so obvious. An organizational change in the Ministry of Defense had formally created the position of national armaments director and elevated General Fabio Moizo to fill it. The United States used the occasion of Ruffini's accession to renew the campaign against Italy's stand on AWACS.[25] Thus, a confluence of events and circumstances had set the stage for a change in Italy's position.

The American Embassy in Rome and General Bowman, both having persisted in the matter, knew of the potential for change. Moizo, a man of vision who immediately understood the merit of AWACS, would press from the inside. The Embassy and

Bowman would lobby from the outside. Brown wrote to Ruffini—at Bowman's suggestion—asking him to reconsider Italy's position. Surely, Brown probed, in an annual defense budget of $4 billion, Italy could find, say, $5 million a year for five years, by which time economic conditions would have improved? Ruffini waivered while Moizo worked at converting Italy's senior military. In addition to more standard arguments, he promised to sponsor having Italy's payments taken from the defense budget before it was proportioned among the uniformed services, thereby effectively removing one major objection. Moizo proselytized, among others, Brigadier General D'Ambrosio, a former college classmate of Ruffini's and a senior member of the minister's personal staff. D'Ambrosio, in turn, coaxed Ruffini. Bowman supplied Moizo with ammunition for Ruffini's skirmish with the cabinet. Under reasonable circumstances, Italy would recoup most of its initial five-year contribution. The Department of Defense recognized the lopsided pattern in American-Italian defense trade; perhaps an agreement waiving buy-national requirements would help.[26]

Moizo and D'Ambrosio flew to Washington to seal the bargain. Italy agreed to pay no more than about $5 million annually through 1983, the amount to be adjusted to include inflation. By no later than 1983 Italy would review its economic situation with a view toward paying the balance of the $100 million share in $10 to $15 million annual increments. For its part the United States would stand with Italy to resist any pressure from other governments for increases in the agreed payment schedule. Though a significant political victory with important psychological importance for all governments, the agreement was grievously flawed from the onset. Even at the high side of the payment schedule, Italy would not pay its last contribution toward acquisition costs until 1988, or as late as three years after all acquisition bills needed to be settled. Why would the United States and Italy strike such an agreement, and why would no other government object to it?

The reasons are neither complex nor mysterious. Almost resigned to Italy's symbolic participation, governments at the time would have embraced any substantial increase in Italy's pledge. And this pledge, offered literally at the eleventh hour, unexpectedly was for a full share. Any number of events over the next few years could lead Italy to increase its annual payments. Besides, the arithmetic of Italy's payments was not the only peculiarity in the program. An accountant might have rejected the financial agreement as unworkable. For his part, Ruffini, a newly vested defense minister, could not possibly know what sum would prove to be the breaking point with the cabinet. His pledge, if nothing else, could be defended as reasonable. Moreover, too great an annual payment very early might suggest to Italy's factional parliament, then considering a sweeping defense budget initiative, that the Ministry of Defense enjoyed surplus funds in its budget.

With Ruffini's letter to Luns on 15 May—three days before the spring meeting of defense ministers—the search for consensus on financial arrangements stood essentially complete. Whether the consensus recommendations would be ratified in capitals, however likely, was, everyone knew, far from certain. How far from certain no one would have guessed.

4. UNCERTAINTIES

On 8 March 1978, Luns signed a covering memorandum formally transmitting the package proposal to Permanent Representatives who, in turn, passed it to the various governments on 30 March. One year had passed since Mulley announced Britain's Nimrod decision, and, to the uninformed critic, NATO had produced only a fragile cost-sharing proposal agreed or footnoted ad referendum by various nations' representatives. Any single government could reject or ignore the proposal and thus significantly damage, if not scuttle, the program. But, to those involved, forging a consensus proposal on AWACS, except for a few details, in one year's time seemed nothing short of remarkable.

Those few details aside, the unity and momentum of the moment seemed to favor success. Alliance unity, at first little more than a catch phrase as applied to NATO AWACS, had become over time an important motivating force that no ally would treat too lightly in considering the proposal. That the call for Alliance solidarity initially substituted for sharper reasoning and more compelling arguments did not matter at that point. Enough allies had willingly picked up on the unity theme to make it a highly relevant and positive consideration. Momentum, however, proved ephemeral because thirteen sets of pressures, priorities, and approval processes in thirteen different capitals required additional time and compromise. And it proved to be that because a consensus on financial arrangements, however central to the program's success, was a far cry from a decision document.

The remainder of 1978 featured a constant state of uncertainty first in one capital, then another, and, on at least one occasion, in all capitals simultaneously. We can probably never know all that happened, but what we do know or can reasonably reconstruct reflects both the fascination and difficulty of NATO's decision to acquire an AWACS force. The episodes highlighted here were either central or particularly instructive or both. Although they occurred more or less simultaneously and influenced one another to varying degrees, this study treats them separately for purposes of readability and comprehension. The reader must therefore overlay the events to savor the delightfully maddening confusion and dynamism of parallel decision making in capitals. The first event spanned the whole of 1978, starting while financial negotiations were still in progress and ending a few weeks after ministers approved the program.

A Precarious Beginning

The computer technology underpinning a standardized AWACS needed to be adapted to the relatively harsh environment of an airplane. The adaptation would take time and money. Consequently, if NATO wanted standardized AWACS starting with the first airplane delivered, and at the advertised price, nations would have to fund the requisite research and development effort well before they formally approved the program.[1] They funded the effort—as it happened, on a frayed shoestring.

On the given assumption that ministers would approve the program before 1 July, the contractor said in January that $5 million for computer adaptation efforts beginning by 1 April 1978 would be sufficient to protect cost and schedule for standardized AWACS. Walsh proposed that minor-share nations each pay identical sums of $50 thousand so as not to prejudice the cost-sharing negotiations then underway. Seven nations agreed. Walsh also proposed that major procurement partners fund the balance. They concurred in a qualified fashion.

Walsh's proposal appeared equitable, but it did not—indeed, could not—account for the political realities of the moment. As a result of earlier contributions (toward preparatory costs) that led to injunctions from their legislatures, Germany and the United States could not fund their shares without prior legislative approval. Neither defense establishment reacted enthusiastically to the prospect of seeking such approval, especially for a small sum, a matter of months before NATO ministers might decide the initiative. Legislatures rightfully might ask for details and, if not satisfied, refuse the request or "suggest" limits or conditions to participation. Either would profoundly influence the program. Besides, would or could the Congress act on a "paltry sum" for NATO AWACS at about the time President Carter submitted a new budget (and the first reflecting his administration's goals) for congressional action? Risks far exceeded potential returns. The same may have been true in Germany, but its problem was part of a much more complex pattern that will be examined presently.

Both nations suggested, therefore, that the Programme Office offer up whatever funds could be comfortably spared from the American and German monies previously contributed. Partly because of this suggestion, but more because Danson simply could not afford politically to get too far out on such an uncertain venture, Canada quietly suggested to Walsh that the Canadian share also be limited to $50 thousand. Walsh agreed and, America's low-key protest to Canada notwithstanding, the suggestion stuck.

As a consequence of these legitimate problems in three capitals, NATO could collectively pledge less than half of the amount required for pacing work on the computer. The contractor obligingly reduced the level of effort to match available funds and quietly kept track of the resultant cost growth for standard AWACS.[2] Equally troublesome, the Programme Office retained just enough operating capital to continue its activities at a bare-bones level for perhaps six months. Worst of all, if defense ministers did not approve the program for a 1 July start, then nations would have to find more money or agree to terminate the computer effort, close out Programme Office activities, and watch program costs mushroom beyond affordability. One should not call the arrangements a gamble. The odds were not that sporting.

The spring 1978 meeting of defense ministers came and went without a decision on AWACS, six weeks really being insufficient time for capitals to review and approve a two-pound document.[3] Moreover, the proposal did not include a completed decision document for ministers' signatures. In light of subsequent problems centering on it, the optimism inherent in the interim funding scheme can best be described as inexplicable. When another delay became apparent, Walsh asked ministers to approve interim funding to protect the program costs and schedule (that is, to continue the computer work) as well as to keep the Programme Office operating. Walsh's scheme called for those six nations scheduled to pay an annual share in the program's first year to advance the $8 million needed for the next three months.[4] His proposal was logical, practical, and, of course, necessary. Unfortunately, it once again flew in the face of the political problems in Bonn, Ottawa, and Washington.

This time, however, the Pentagon did not automatically reject the risk of asking the Congress to lift its restriction on NATO AWACS funding. Earlier circumstances had changed significantly. When Luns moved the package proposal to capitals for review and approval, an action that by itself carried political meaning, Brown wisely sent copies to the Congress. The pacing research and development effort had begun more or less on time with contributions from ten NATO governments. Defense ministers had recently agreed to continue interim funding for the time they thought capitals needed to complete their respective decision processes. The Netherlands and Luxembourg, stalwart supporters both, had already paid their shares of the new interim funding requirement. And the Congress, although its work on the budget was far from finished, had at least digested the President's recommendations.

Still, the Office of the Secretary of Defense did not decide the question without first carefully reviewing alternatives. An official in the General Counsel's office pointed out that the language of the legislative restriction left a narrow legal opening for exploitation. The Congress specifically restricted only the $15.7 million authorized and appropriated in fiscal year 1978 for NATO AWACS from expenditure or obligation until NATO signed a purchase contract. Perhaps the Department could use some of the other $3.8 billion Congress authorized and appropriated for research, development, test, and evaluation without relevant restriction.[5] Imperfect legislative language or not, no American defense official seriously considered playing games with the Congress on such an important matter. The Air Force looked for "old money" that might be used—that is, AWACS research, development, test, and evaluation money authorized and appropriated prior to fiscal year 1978 still carried on the books.[6] There was none to be spared.

With no alternatives in sight, the Department searched for a feasible approach to the Congress. It would not be a simple matter. The Congress adheres to its own way of doing business and, in this instance, congressional approval would require a change in Public Law 96–79.[7] Then Dame Fortune smiled. The House of Representatives had already passed its version of the Fiscal Year 1979 Defense Authorization Bill, but the Senate version had yet to reach the floor for a vote. A floor amendment might work. The restriction had originated in the Senate; moreover, the bill to which the amendment would be attached was for defense procurement. Both factors were highly relevant. After hurried consultations between Defense and the Senate at staff levels and assurances of support—the latter due in no small way to the contractor's behind-the-scenes lobbying on the Hill—Brown wrote to Senator Stennis (D-Miss) asking for help.

Senator Nunn (D-Ga), co-author of key legislation on NATO standardization, agreed to sponsor an amendment from the floor.[8] He and his staff so carefully coordinated the effort with key senators from both parties that, by the time he rose to speak, the formality of a vote was all that remained. Brown said he needed $4 million; the Senate removed restrictions on all of the money.[9]

But the Senate vote was, of course, a long way from a change in law or the provision of desperately needed funds. The measure would have to be considered by the Senate-House Conference Committee (on defense authorizations), perhaps return to both floors for a second vote, and be sent to the President for signature. Then in another few days to a week for administrative processing, the money could be disbursed. With luck, only three months would have passed. But how could the contractor's bills be paid in the meantime?

The obvious answers were either to not pay the bills or to "ask" the contractor not to present them. Easy enough, except the Department of Defense cannot ask a contractor to work unless the Department holds funds authorized and appropriated or otherwise approved by Congress for such work.[10] It did not have any. The prime contractor, Boeing Aerospace, well aware of the situation because of Walsh's lobbying, offered to continue the work at risk. A relieved Department of Defense said nothing, since it could not. NATO's Programme Office agreed.

The scene—albeit with less drama—played a second time a few months later. The three-month extension of interim funding proved insufficient for ministers to approve the full program. Accordingly, Walsh called for a third increment of funding. By that time, however, the two European governments funding the second increment announced that their contributions for a third would be withheld until the three major procurement partners funded their shares. Most understood the true meaning. Why should they assume a risk when Canada and Germany would not? That Canada and Germany could not pay for valid political reasons—and Germany perhaps for legal reasons as well—did not impress them. They suffered their own political problems. Thus, it fell to the United States to carry the interim effort. Brown wrote another letter to the Chairmen of the Armed Services Committees asking for $6 million. Neither objected, probably because of Brown's solid reputation with the Congress and because of professional courtesy to a senior cabinet official. Certainly, the Secretary could offer no compelling argument in favor of additional funding under the circumstances.

The precarious beginning of the NATO AWACS program—nine months of interim funding for critically important pacing work—reveals something about the psychology and politics of Alliance decision making. Few governments were willing to accept the political risk of being the first to step forward with substantial funding support for such an expensive, controversial, and unprecedented program. Getting all to step forward simultaneously may have been an obvious answer, but it would also have been a naive one. The North Atlantic Alliance, or any other group of diverse individuals responsible to different and multiple constituencies, does not work that way. One member, perhaps two or three, must take the lead—either openly or behind the scenes—and suffer the grief and sacrifices either approach can confer. Such is the obligation and price of leadership.

Historically, the leaders in NATO have been few. With respect to AWACS, two started and others joined in at key junctures, but only one traveled the entire course. If Germany had undertaken a leadership role at senior levels as well, that initiative no doubt would have encountered much less delay. AWACS would not have suffered a precarious beginning.

But then the German defense establishment suffered its own set of political problems, the roots of which America, and perhaps others, viewed as an uncertain commitment. That particular analysis of commitment confused effect with cause. The uncertain commitment in Germany was driven in large measure by the new defense minister's understandable reluctance to spend considerable amounts of his precious political capital for an American initiative blessed by Leber but resisted by other important elements in the German Government.

An Inherited Political Problem

The defense portfolio in Germany's recent past has held promise for many incumbents. They used the position—Helmut Schmidt successfully—to launch an election campaign for the chancellorship. The relationship is understandable. Defense consistently overshadows other cabinet posts for reasons of budget, scope, and difficulty of the management effort required. It plays a dominant role in most foreign policy considerations, and public visibility is high. Dr. Hans Apel, brilliant and ambitious in equal measure, understood the relationship well when he handed over his Minister of Finance portfolio to replace Leber. The new job represented both an opportunity and a challenge for someone aspiring to be chancellor.

Apel could begin by avoiding the "mistakes" of his predecessor.[11] Leber, a charter member so to speak of the Social Democrats, had rather consistently taken positions somewhat out of step with his party colleagues. He pressed for higher defense spending when his party's campaign platform called for no increases and he faithfully supported American political leadership in NATO when the left wing of the Social Democrats preferred to maintain a discreet distance. In short, he acted too much like a Christian Democrat on defense issues. In consequence, he displeased many in both parties. Moreover, he was loyal to a fault to his generals—championing their causes and defending occasional excesses.

As a first step toward impressing the ministry with his quite different style, Apel asked the senior staff to review with him the status of all major acquisition programs. Altenburg presented the case for NATO AWACS, not yet a procurement program, certainly not in the five-year budget plan—and, those present suspected, not one of Apel's favorites. However, Altenburg's presentation, or perhaps some thought-provoking information in the presentation, gave Apel pause. He looked to the others for comments.

Silence.

Who among the seniors wanted to be the first to speak in favor of AWACS when the new defense minister reportedly thought it an extravagance? The service chiefs shared the thought to the extent that they did not wish to sacrifice other programs for it. The Army would rather spend its money on antitank helicopters, field howitzers, more tanks, air defense missiles, or armored personnel carriers. The

Navy, sized and built for coastal defense, viewed AWACS' future maritime surveillance capability with open skepticism. Besides, the Navy might lose, or have to reduce, its maritime air patrol assets. The Air Force thought its Low Altitude Radar System, sited along the border and filling gaps here and there, good enough to redress the surveillance and tracking deficiencies of the Air Defense Ground Environment. Who needed AWACS, at that price, for 15 minutes' additional warning time? Furthermore, AWACS radar range exceeded the combat radius of many German Air Force interceptors. Why buy a system that can "see" farther than you can fly?

Dr. Karl Schnell, a four-star Army officer who retired to serve as Leber's deputy, moved to Altenburg's defense. "The airplane is phenomenal and the program laced with political understandings and commitments," he offered. Hans Eberhard, Germany's national armaments director, noted that no one could deny the technological benefits of AWACS. Apel asked about German funding for the program. The silence that followed apparently settled the question, at least for the moment, in the defense minister's mind. Why sponsor a controversial initiative for which there was uneven support and no money?

A few weeks later, Apel publicly proposed postponing the NATO AWACS program two years for budgetary reasons. Privately, he began taking soundings for support after his senior staff reminded him Leber had committed Germany in principle to the program on the basis of the Federal Security Council's endorsement. Initial soundings were not encouraging. His successor at Finance, Hans Matthoefer, repeated to him what he and

Schmidt had told Leber a year earlier. The Ministry of Defense would have to fund AWACS from within approved spending levels. Neither did staff informational presentations to the Bundestag's Defense Committee on 12 April 1978 lend much comfort. Among other complaints signalling future Bundestag demands, the Defense Committee wanted to know about compensation for Germany's share. What about the "two-way street" in defense trade it asked?[12] The Bundestag would not be stampeded on AWACS.

Apel's public statements did not go down well in Washington. Brown wrote to point out that a two-year delay for NATO AWACS represented an unworkable suggestion. Program costs would escalate beyond the level of affordability if NATO did not protect the standardized AWACS option. And, Brown cautioned, the United States would not proceed unilaterally with the development effort. Others complained as well, apparently with some effect. Sometime later that spring, Helmut Schmidt privately told Apel to "find the money."[13]

Apel had inherited a difficult political position for which he would have to devise a solution. He chose to turn Leber's legacy to his advantage. From then on, he painted AWACS as a Leber commitment that he had no choice but to honor. The tactic was clever. He could push it and simultaneously maintain some distance, provided he did not push too hard or fast. If his Social Democrat colleagues in the Bundestag repudiated NATO AWACS, that repudiation would largely be of Leber's commitment. And it would be difficult to repudiate it without challenging the judgment of the Social Democrat elders who endorsed Leber's appointment as

Minister of Defense. When, on the other hand, the Bundestag approved Germany's participation in the program, the credit would largely and correctly belong to Apel. And if the Christian Democrat minority railed against one-way traffic on the "two-way street," Apel would oblige them as well with concessions wrung from the Americans. AWACS need not be the liability it was for Leber.

But AWACS could be a liability for Apel if the Bundestag's formal hearings on German participation followed the pattern of the 12 April presentation. The commitment might be Leber's, but the responsibility for maneuvering AWACS through the legislative process fell to Apel. Next time, therefore, he needed an air-tight case—no loose ends, no unanswered questions, and no Bundestag demands uncovered. The preparatory work would take time, particularly for an inexperienced, but politically ambitious, defense minister considering dozens of difficult security issues. A few capitals, including Washington, still nervous about Apel's public pronouncements, incorrectly viewed his tactic as having a deeper, more troublesome, meaning.

As for a German share of the interim funding effort, Apel dared not approach the Bundestag before he was ready. Others would have to carry the burden, since he would not or could not budge on this point. Even much later, when a portion of Germany's industrial collaboration was at stake, he would not move.[14] German contractors proceeded at their own risk to preserve the industrial collaboration package for the Federal Republic.

Actions in the United States were not particularly helpful to Apel, who had settled on economic compensation as his leading argument for

AWACS. The bilateral Memorandum of Agreement on the American Army's purchase of German-manufactured vehicles held great promise, but had yielded precious few contracts. Negotiations for the American Army's purchase of an upgraded telephone system from the Deutsches Bundespost had bogged down, and the tank gun agreement showed signs of coming apart. (There seemed to be a misunderstanding over royalties and data rights as well as licensed production arrangements and export prerogatives.) As a final straw, the House Appropriations Committee zeroed funding for the German tank gun. In each instance, senior American defense officials had been able to repair the damage, but had not been able to dispel the feelings of suspicion and cynicism held by many influential German parliamentarians.

By November 1978, Apel felt ready. He was also out of time. He could point to the promise of economic offsets for the whole of Germany's $560 million acquisition share as well as for Germany's share of AWACS' annual operating and support costs.[15] The former had been particularly difficult to pin down in convincing fashion. On top of delay after delay, the Americans would not agree to count their recent procurement initiatives in Germany solely as compensation for AWACS, even though they rushed—unsuccessfully, as it happened—to implement the initiatives to accommodate Apel's political needs. The Americans insisted, rather, that the initiatives stood alone, defensible as cost-effective acquisitions tendered in the interest of achieving a more equitable balance in defense trade.[16]

Apel could show no important purchase contracts for German-manufactured equipment, only open-ended agreements and written assurances from Brown, but he could point to other governments' positive support. Apel would not have to describe for Bundestag committees the obvious political implications of Germany's failing to carry its share of the common burden. Unfortunately he, like Leber, did not enjoy the advantage of arguing that AWACS would meet a national military requirement. Germany's military service chiefs, recently subdued by Apel's management style and Schmidt's support for AWACS, apparently could not bring themselves to say the Federal Republic needed it. The case would necessarily rest on NATO solidarity and economic compensation.

Apel's deputy, Dr. Karl Schnell, took the lead in defending NATO AWACS to the Bundestag. It proved an eleventh-hour defense. The Social Democrat majority in the Defense Committee delayed the hearings two weeks to 28 November, or eight days before defense ministers would meet to decide the program, perhaps slipping the hearings to await the outcome of the tank gun misunderstandings. Germany's legislative calendar influenced events elsewhere as well. Until German support was assured—an eventuality appearing less than certain at the time—few Allied defense establishments would move to secure parliamentary approval for the program.

The Bundestag completed its deliberations in three days. On 28 November 1978, the Defense Committee voted in favor of NATO AWACS by a margin of 24-3 and, two days later, the Budget Committee passed the measure by a vote of 24-8-1. Lopsided voting margins notwithstanding, Apel had scored only a qualified victory. Both committees challenged the credibility of the compensation package by, in effect, saying, "show us American purchase contracts for German equipment."[17] Moreover, they openly held Germany's share hostage to delivery of the promised compensation package. Given events over the summer and fall, one can understand why. In a final minor ignominy, Schnell received more credit than Apel for maneuvering the program through the Bundestag.[18]

The Decision Document

The decision document for defense ministers, called in the verbal shorthand of the AWACS program a Multilateral Memorandum of Understanding (MMOU), was in a legal sense the least important of the three principal documents required to implement it.[19] But it was the most important in almost every other respect. It set out the terms and conditions of each government's political commitment, even if those commitments were largely defined in non-political terms and carefully hedged. It would serve as the future touchstone for program disputes between participating governments as they tried to implement a program crippled by constrictive footnotes and reservations that none wanted to be the first to remove. And the Memorandum, in any event, mattered more than the other two decision documents simply because, without its approval by defense ministers, governments need not worry about the other two. It was, in sum, the decision document for NATO AWACS. Haggling over its contents led to delay and uncertainty.

More by default than design, governments sent a variety of specialists to negotiate and draft the Memorandum. Being talented specialists, they tended to view the world as if its finite parts—particularly the ones they knew best—were more important than the whole. They enjoyed neither antecedent agreements to make their task lighter nor much routine help from national financial experts who seemed preoccupied with the more fundamental and nagging political problems of 1978. Not surprisingly, therefore, progress on the Multilateral Memorandum of Understanding inched forward even after nations had tentatively agreed on financial terms.

Such usually, perhaps always, is the problem with negotiating and drafting a complex agreement for which neither a model nor universal commitment exists. Where should one start—with details that, once compiled, dictate the form and substance of the whole—or with a vision of the whole for which supporting details can be found or forced to fit? Both must of course be considered in balance, but it is indeed a rare negotiator who can work equally well with detail and vision. When men of vision addressed NATO AWACS issues, they found solutions by largely ignoring the pesky details that could (and would) in time jeopardize the solutions. When specialists addressed the issues, they worshipped detail while, in effect, largely ignoring both the calendar and the notion of accommodation. A perfect solution too late would be no solution at all.

Over time, however, a negotiating pattern emerged leading to progress on the Memorandum. Specialists attended the monthly negotiating sessions, stated their convictions or instructions, listened carefully to others' convictions or instructions, and reported the results back home. Sometimes their seniors changed instructions as a result and sometimes they wrote to counterparts in other capitals to resolve issues blocking progress.[20] Cumbersome and time-consuming, the system pleased almost no one, but it worked—barely. The NATO staff submitted a tentatively negotiated Multilateral Memorandum of Understanding to capitals about two weeks before defense ministers would meet to sign or reject it.

For those defense establishments needing to circulate the Memorandum through other government agencies for approval, the two weeks under normal circumstances would have been insufficient. In the case of the United States, for example, the Air Force staff, the Office of the Secretary of Defense, the Office of Management and Budget, the National Security Council, and the Department of State had to review and approve (or at least not reject) the document for signature. (The Department of Commerce probably should have as well, in light of the technology transfer and export license requirements in the agreement.) The approval process concluded just in time. The Under Secretary of State for Security Assistance, Science, and Technology cabled an approval, the night before ministers were to meet, for Brown to sign. Other governments' approval processes varied, of course, but those whose processes required interdepartmental review of the Memorandum apparently encountered similar difficulties—some more than others since only an English language copy was available. Indeed, late receipt of the Memorandum proved to be one of the major factors leading to the ultimate uncertainty. The week before ministers were scheduled to meet, prospects for approval collapsed.

Before that drama unfolded, however, negotiation of details revealed a bit of the ingenuity and perplexity encountered in bargaining sessions between allies. Governments encountered perplexing situations and needed ingenious work-arounds largely because of someone's decision—or perhaps no one's decision to the contrary—to treat the Memorandum more as a legal contract than a political instrument. Goodwill and diplomatic imperatives between sovereign allies might be good enough to "enforce" the agreement, but not good enough to lave certain "legal" details unattended. Yet, on a few occasions when those details appeared to impinge on the prerogatives of political sovereigns, the document's language turned disturbingly vague.

At some point toward the end of 1978 a need arose to accommodate the possibility that one party or another might not be able to sign the Memorandum. Aside from the political implications for those allies with a stated need for NATO-wide participation, such an event posed a political problem with self-imposed legalistic overtones. If the Memorandum listed all governments as parties to the agreement, and one government could or would not sign, would the agreement still be binding?

The political answer in a perfect world is relatively easy: yes, it is binding if the signatories wish it to be binding. One political answer in our imperfect world is a bit less certain: it may or may not be binding but, if all save one sign and proceed, then what incentive does the non-signatory have to sign later? The apparent legal answer, and the one representatives chose to view as the correct one, yields yet another result. No, it is not binding until all listed parties sign. This answer, once identified, posed another choice. Should the Memorandum list all governments or, if not, which governments? The clever solution to this unproductive exercise was to list the signatory governments in only one place and then refer to that throughout the document. The one place could be filled in sometime shortly before ministers actually signed the Memorandum. One can suppose every protracted negotiation produces at least one false issue that wastes energies and talents, but this particular one did more. Those who worried about it questioned the integrity of NATO members.

Deliberations on withdrawal and termination provisions in the document took a different tack. Here, where legalistic precision may have been appropriate, some representatives argued, successfully, for statements of good intentions. Those arguing this line had a good point. Once a government formally agreed to share AWACS' costs, it could scarcely terminate that agreement unilaterally and preemptively without calling into question its reliability in other important Alliance defense matters. Political reality though it may have been, statements of good intentions brought little comfort at all to those early-paying governments who feared getting stuck and no comfort at all to the contractor, particularly since the Department of Defense had already agreed to waive prepayment of termination liability costs. The contractor would have to wait to complain, however, because the NATO staff had labelled negotiation results as "commercially sensitive."[21]

Differences in political processes within governments also played an important role in sustaining anxieties and uncertainties during the negotiation of details. America's federal system, with its balance-of-power arrangements that lead to internal adversarial relationships, seldom ceases to dismay allies.

They strike a bargain with a political entity they think represents the United States Government only later to witness the Congress wreak havoc by either failing to sustain the bargain with funds or a ratifying vote, or by taking months to act. Senior American officials, on the other hand, puzzle over the paralysis of some coalition parliamentary governments where tomorrow's vote can mean starting over with a new counterpart. Both sides of course have studied the institutional arrangements within the other's political system. Neither, at times, however, seems really to understand either how those arrangements work or why otherwise intelligent people would retain them. With respect to NATO AWACS negotiations, some Allies wanted more than assurances from the Department of Defense that the United States (that is, the Congress) would hold up its end of the bargain. The Multilateral Memorandum of Understanding, as negotiated, required unusual business arrangements, an unprecedented exception to the Arms Export Control Act, and an American share right at the upper limits of acceptability. The Congress could reject any feature, and thus force the allies either to start over or terminate the initiative.

Allied defense establishments had driven a hard bargain with the Department of Defense. Success, in this instance, led to uncertainty. Would the Congress go along? American defense officials' written and verbal caveats nurtured the uncertainty. After each provision of the Memorandum calling for an exception to American law, defense negotiators necessarily added a written caution to the effect that implementation required congressional approval. Moreover, American negotiators so frequently added verbal warnings of possible adverse congressional reactions to the host of concessions wanted by the allies that some began to believe them. Germany's Bundestag, in particular, was sufficiently concerned to condition German participation on congressional acceptance of business arrangements in the Memorandum.[22] No one at the time, including the Americans, could know the Congress would approve the program, as negotiated, with minimal fanfare.

Still another set of uncertainties welled up from what appeared to be eleventh-hour realizations in some capitals that other participants might be getting a better deal. This realization, or at least actions stemming from it, probably would never have occurred if NATO AWACS had not been so politicized. Concessions that made little sense, "compensation" packages, deferred payments, and other political accommodations, however essential to the program's success, apparently led some governments to conclude they were, in effect, being penalized for their straightforward support of AWACS. And they were.

The Dutch, for example, had strongly supported AWACS since their "conversion" in 1976. They accepted the "fresh start" compromise on acquisition shares even though it increased their share by 10 percent, and they had agreed to pay a share during the early years of acquisition even though they too suffered a tight defense budget. They did not fight Germany on the location of the main operating base, even if airplanes operating from it would thunder over Dutch homes. The Dutch had supported the compromise on shares of AWACS' annual operating and support costs even though the compromise increased their share, and they had shared interim funding needs when others held back. For all of this, the Dutch stood to gain almost no economic return.

Whatever its motivation, the Netherlands moved at the last minute to secure an economic benefit. It chose the Programme Office, which had been operating from a temporary suite of offices at NATO Headquarters.[23] The Dutch could solve two problems with one solution by offering a handsome new facility specifically built, half with Dutch money and half with common funds, for a NATO military headquarters that never moved to the Netherlands. To secure their choice, the Dutch moved quietly to line up support beforehand and then placed a reservation on the relevant document to keep open the question of the Programme Office's location until they could prevail in a more formal manner.[24] The Belgians resisted, of course, since it was their economic benefit at stake. However, they enjoyed little political leverage under the circumstances that would unfold at the ministerial session. Those, in fact, began to unfold a little more than a week before ministers would meet.

A Final Flurry

The ultimate uncertainty started innocently enough. NATO's Permanent Representatives met to discuss the upcoming Defense Planning Committee meeting. Several representatives complained that late receipt of the Multilateral Memorandum of Understanding·did not permit adequate staffing prior to the defense minister's meeting. Their ministers, therefore, would not be able to sign the document until later in December. On hearing this, Ambassador Schuurmans, Belgium's Permanent

Representative, announced to his colleagues that one of the consequences of his government's having fallen recently would be acting Minister Vanden Boeynant's inability to agree to share NATO AWACS acquisition costs or to sign the Memorandum. Neither the fall of Belgium's factionalized government nor Schuurmans' announcement on AWACS came as a particular surprise to the assembled ambassadors. But what happened next did.

Before exchanges ended a matter of minutes later, the house of cards holding up NATO AWACS had collapsed. Portugal's Permanent Representative, picking up on Schuurmans' remarks, said his defense minister faced a similar problem. The newly formed Portuguese Cabinet had not yet been formally approved by the strife-torn parliament and, even if it soon were, NATO AWACS could hardly be its first order of business. Whereupon, Hardy responded that if Belgium and Portugal could not sign, neither would Canada. Germany's Charge d'Affaires seconded the notion. Others joined the chorus, each with his own notion of tempo and tune. The long-lost momentum had been found again—only this time it was accelerating in the wrong direction.

No one present—perhaps least of all Hardy—intended to terminate AWACS. Each had simply spoken the truth. Belgium had no government. Portugal had a brand-new government facing dreadful economic problems and the lingering aftermath of a brief flirtation with communism. Canada and Germany had long stated their political need for all nations to support the program financially. The larger truth, perhaps grasped in its stark entirety only by the United States, was that another delay meant the end of the program. It could not be otherwise. Who would carry a fourth increment of interim funding under the circumstances? With or without interim funding, escalating costs would crush the fragile agreements reached thus far. There comes a time when one must cut losses—whether they are financial, political, or emotional.

Deputy Secretary General Petrignani, sitting in for Luns, tried to limit the damage by calling for a meeting the next day. Time can be an ally among allies. Petrignani shared with Maynard Glitman, the United States Deputy Chief of Mission at NATO, and probably other representatives, his notion of a compromise he would offer. Those defense ministers who could sign the Memorandum on 6 December 1978 would do so and the others, who complained of insufficient time to staff the document, could sign as soon as possible thereafter. The Memorandum would not become valid until all but Belgium and Portugal, the two governments with implacable political problems, had signed. Few suffered any illusions that the compromise, even if it were acceptable to all, would result in a viable program.

Two "immediate" cables arrived in Washington on the same afternoon of the disastrous meeting. One, from Glitman, reluctantly recommended Washington's support for Petrignani's compromise as the one workable alternative to seeing three years' work go down the drain. Ironically, the second cable, from Bonn, reported the Bundestag Defense Committee's favorable vote on AWACS.

Only a handful of people in Washington considered fighting for what appeared to be a failed proposition. What could possibly be done in a week that could not be achieved in more than a year? But the Office of International Security Affairs did not suffer defeat gladly nor did the State Department's European Affairs Bureau which agreed to speed along the flurry of cables. A week can be forever.

As a first step, McGiffert's office asked Glitman to seek a delay in the meeting Petrignani had called. Petrignani and Luns, who had hurried back into the picture, agreed to Glitman's request for delay. At the same time, McGiffert asked Brown to lend his considerable prestige to the effort, attaching to his request a list of four immediate actions aimed at the core of the problem. Brown agreed to send personal cables to Portugal's new minister of defense, to Apel, and to Ruffini. He also agreed to call Danson in the morning. The Permanent Representatives from each of these governments had, of course, played a key role in the outcome of that day's meeting in Brussels.

All four messages focused on the need to sign the Multilateral Memorandum of Understanding at the rapidly approaching ministerial session lest the program slip away. To each message, he added personal touches relating to the problems with AWACS in that capital. Brown also asked Apel to use his considerable powers of persuasion with the Italians and the Portuguese. Germany's financial assistance to those countries would no doubt lend additional weight to Apel's approach. In appropriate instances, Brown told each what he was attempting to do with the others. Events blurred over the next few days. McGiffert flew to Brussels on 29 November to do what he could to muster support and shore up potential breaches. Ruffini asked for a bilateral meeting with Brown just prior to the ministers' meeting and he agreed. (Brown thought Ruffini might need last minute moral support.) American embassies here and there pitched in, as they so often had during the preceding months of tribulation, to reinforce approaches and gauge the depth of resistance. Brown called Danson who agreed to try to speed the review process for the Memorandum. Apel contacted both the Italians and the Portuguese with some effect. Based on McGiffert's reporting from Brussels and London, Brown sent out another batch of personalized cables to London, Copenhagen, and Ankara, and agreed to meet privately with Defense Minister dos Santos of Portugal. McGiffert's staff dispatched a list of arguments for Glitman to use during the rescheduled meeting of Permanent Representatives while Brown sent a reinforcing cable to Ruffini and a follow-up cable to Danson. Charles Duncan, Brown's deputy, called Mulley's deputy to dampen his staff's recommendation not to sign the Memorandum. Finally, Brown agreed to meet privately with Mulley. And so it went.

Permanent Representatives met again on 30 November. Technically, they were meeting as the North Atlantic Council in permanent session rather than the Defense Planning Committee in permanent session. Luns presided. Being only vaguely aware of the flurry of cables and telephone calls from Washington and even less aware of their impact, he offered the Petrignani compromise. Glitman immediately argued against anything other than full signatures on the Memorandum at the ministerial meeting. Support not yet having firmed in capitals, ambassadors reacted politely, but without much change in their positions of two days' earlier. Glitman persisted—persistence sometimes being as important as logic, delay, or the other tactics routinely employed by representatives. Canada persisted as well. Hardy argued for a "Minute of Agreement" in lieu of the Multilateral Memorandum of Understanding, thinking such an instrument insufficient to begin the program while staffing of the Memorandum continued in capitals. Representatives chewed on that one for a while. Some thought an agreed Minute sufficiently legal to undertake financial commitments; others thought not. Glitman stood firm— the psychology, not the legalities, of the decision instrument dictated his stance.

The momentum against signing had spent itself. Ambassadors had shifted to discussing what and when, not whether, ministers would sign. A few supported Glitman, a few Hardy, and a few others supported the Petrignani compromise. While they searched for common ground, Pauls received word, and passed it to his colleagues, that the Bundestag Budget Committee had approved AWACS. Apel, he speculated, might be able to sign the Multilateral Memorandum of Understanding after all. Pauls' fortuitous announcement and Glitman's unyielding stance combined with the underlying, but temporarily derailed, commitment to turn momentum around. Choices narrowed to two. The Petrignani compromise slipped quietly into oblivion.

Ministers would decide the question. Luns agreed to place the Memorandum before them for signature. Canada's Minute of Agreement recommendation would, over American protests, serve as a fallback. Not satisfied with what it viewed as an all-or-nothing-at-all choice, Washington quietly maneuvered for an in-between choice. If incomplete staffing were a problem in Bonn, London, Ottawa, and Rome, perhaps ministers could sign the Memorandum with the explicit condition it would not be binding for seven days. Under rules of the "silence procedure," if no defense minister took action during that time to void his signature, the Memorandum would go into effect. Lest it appear disingenuous for its firm stand with Permanent Representatives, Washington arranged for some other party to suggest the in-between choice if it became necessary.

Brown and his party left for Brussels in the late afternoon of 4 December. Over the last several days, uncertainties of the preceding months had succumbed to near certain failure, which in turn had moved over for a return of uncertainties. This time, however, mere uncertainties proved strangely comforting. An action checklist in Brown's book of briefs nicely captured the prospects for NATO AWACS.

Action Checklist for National Positions on NATO AWACS

No nation will want to bear the burden of responsibility for the demise of the program, even though several nations have special interests they are pressing as events converge toward the December DPC (Defense Planning Committee). The following is a checklist of actions taken or actions needed to persuade ministers to sign the Multinational Memorandum of Understanding (MMOU) at the DPC meeting.

US. MMOU now contains clauses that recognize our requirement for congressional approval. MMOU has been staffed through DoD. State expects to complete Circular 175 action by 5 December. OMB and NCS concur.

FRG. Cabinet and Bundestag Committees have approved the program; however, the Minister of Finance believes that Apel cannot sign until the FRG's 1979 budget is approved. Accordingly, Apel is prepared only to make a strongly positive statement at DPC in lieu of signing the MMOU. McGiffert and Glitman will arrange for SecDef telephone call to Apel between 0900-0930, 5 December, in attempt to change FRG position. If Apel will not change his government's position, the house of cards will probably collapse. Apel is not aware of last minute support among nations for signing the MMOU. Stress Canadian position to him.

Italy. Has formally requested parliamentary approval for funds per MOD Ruffini's agreement with Secretary Brown and SYG Luns. This agreement is explicitly recognized in the MMOU (Annex G). Late word that Ruffini will sign, but he needs reassurance during bilateral with SecDef at 0930, 5 December.

Norway. The Cabinet has approved the program. Can sign the MMOU if the proposal has been sent to parliament for ratification (even though ratification not provided); will sign if others do, but will not be out in front.

Luxembourg. Funding already approved. Will sign.

Canada. Cabinet approved Canadian participation on 30 November. Danson said he would sign if all others except Belgium and Portugal sign. Canadians favor a "Minute of Agreement" rather than signing the MMOU.

Denmark. Probably would sign the MMOU at the DPC if most others do, but signature will be subject to parliamentary confirmation. SecDef asked Sogaard to sign, noting that Danish concern with payment schedule (do not want to pay until 1982) has been accommodated in the MMOU.

Turkey. Informal reports indicate Turks are planning to support the program. Probably will sign MMOU at the DPC if all others do, but uncertain. Concerns with Operations and Support cost share have been accommodated with last minute revisions to the MMOU. Overflight rights issue with Greece is unresolved; we should press to have the issue footnoted for further review and approval by the Council. (Note overflight rights is in Section III, three paras of which have already been placed under reservation by the Dutch—suggest adding para 6, Section III to Dutch footnote.)

The Netherlands. Have raised last minute issues with NAPMA location and environmental (noise pollution) compensation. Uncertain whether Scholten will sign the MMOU at the DPC if neither of these issues at least appears to be moving in favor of the Dutch. They probably will fall off the noise pollution issue if NAPMA is located in Brunssum. SecDef letter asking to keep the question of NAPMA open until 31 March may not have been received in time. McGiffert, in checking this out, will point out that Dutch must then be prepared to increase cost shares proportionately to cover Belgian share, since the loss of NAPMA will keep Belgium out of the program. On noise pollution issue, we should agree to study the problem with a view towards taking ministerial decision on it at May DPC meeting. (FYI. Dutch law relevant to this issue has not been passed yet. END FYI) Ambassador Barkman will recommend to Scholten that Dutch sign if there is a consensus on moving NAPMA to Brunssum. The US should support the Brunssum move if all others do.

Portugal. Expected to support the program during the DPC; however, cannot be expected to make significant financial commitment given current economic and financial problems. SecDef letter to dos Santos worked to persuade Portuguese to sign. Dos Santos wants a bilateral to discuss this matter further—possibly on the margins of lunch, 5 December.

UK. Uncertain whether Mulley will sign the MMOU because staffing not complete. Impact of SecDef letter to Mulley and Duncan call to Gilbert unknown. Will still provide its share of funds. Mulley wants a bilateral to discuss the MMOU—UK has offered room after lunch on 5 December.

Belgium. Unable to sign the MMOU since she will have only a transitional government at the time of the DPC meeting. Expected to approve the Charter. Belgium wants the NAPMA in Brussels, but will not or cannot say that the reason is related to its eventual participation. SecDef to Vanden Boeynants and Vance to Simonet letters did not lead to change in Belgian position.

Greece. Continues to express concern over the cost sharing formula which it views as inequitable. Probably will sign the MMOU after the DPC meeting if concerns about offset have been accommodated and Turkish changes to the MMOU are acceptable.

France. Latest reports indicate that CFM-56 re-engining option is no longer operative and that the French will not decide on the question of an airborne early warning capability until later. Want no publicity on approval of the Charter.

The stage was set for ministers' approval. There was no time left for a dress rehearsal.

5. IN MINISTERIAL SESSION

Conference Room 16 at NATO Headquarters is surprisingly austere in both design and appointments. A lofty ceiling, a swath of wood panelling high on one end, national flags, and a heavy, multi-sectioned oblong table for forty-five are the sole concessions to ceremony. It is a functional room for an Alliance whose functional utility moderates the political differences among members. Only when ministers and their senior advisors crowd the table does the room come alive with an air of anticipation, excitement, and ceremony.

NATO AWACS stood as the third item on the defense ministers' agenda. The two topics—each more ritual than substance—preceding AWACS would consume enough of the first day's abbreviated morning session to allow one round of statements on AWACS before a recess for lunch. A buffet in the Salon des Ambassadeurs would thus provide an opportunity for brief private exchanges and last-minute bargaining. Ministers and their aides would put the time to good use.

December 5th

Luns opened the discussion on AWACS by noting that conditions would never again be as favorable for a decision as they were at the moment.[1] The Americans and others had, of course, informed him that the known major obstacles identified in recent days appeared to have been largely surmounted. Nor, in any case, could further delay be accommodated, he observed. In light of these favorable conditions, Luns continued, he trusted defense ministers could now agree to take those actions required to implement the program. The first of these actions would be signing the Multilateral Memorandum of Understanding.

But first, he added, ministers needed to consider the question of locating the Programme Office either in Brussels, Belgium, or Brunssum, the Netherlands. If ministers agreed to Brunssum, Luns probed, then some adjustments in costs might be necessary since financial plans assumed a Brussels location. Luns' veiled remark perhaps reflected the dilemma posed by the Netherlands' last-minute claim to economic benefits. The wisdom of the moment, based largely on past experience, held that Belgium would find it politically difficult to share program costs without some offsetting economic benefit. On the other hand, the Dutch certainly enjoyed at least an equal claim to the benefit, and probably a more justifiable one in light of the circumstances. But if the Dutch were willing to compromise, perhaps some other equally attractive tenant could be found for the Brunssum facility. And if the Dutch could not compromise, then they should recognize, and perhaps share the responsibility for, the financial implications of Belgium's non-participation.

Scholten, responding first, all but settled the matter. The Netherlands' desire to host the Programme Office, he offered, derived primarily from a political and economic need to provide the citizens of Zuid-Limburg some visible benefit from the program. Their homes, 2,300 of them he estimated, were located precisely under the noisiest part of the flight pattern from the AWACS' main operating base at Geilenkirchen, a German airfield on the Dutch border. Even with the Programme Office in Brunssum, Scholten continued, NATO nations ought to share the expense of sound-proofing these homes to comply with Dutch noise pollution standards. In any event, he insisted, the location of the Programme Office could not be separated from the larger question of Dutch participation in the program. Finally, he challenged, how could a NATO-owned facility cost more than a leased office in Brussels? He had deftly deflected the question Luns had really asked.

Luns retreated on the cost question and invited other comments, because few seemed much in the mood to pursue a distraction. Belgium explained its offer to host the management organization still stood even though signing the Memorandum was not possible. Brown signalled support for the Dutch location. Germany's Apel did the same, but added that perhaps Permanent Representatives could decide the question later. Luns got the message. With only scant pause for transition to the heart of the matter, he asked, "Who is ready to sign?"

Brown answered the call with a brief speech. He reviewed the political and practical reasons why ministers needed to take the final and decisive step that day or the next. He seemed to imply that further delay would spell the end of NATO AWACS. As for the matter of parliamentary ratification or approval, which he knew some ministers including himself did not yet have, Brown suggested that the phrase "subject to the availability of funds" in the first section of the Memorandum should permit all ministers to sign. That particular stock bureaucratic phrase—misunderstood, if not distrusted by many Europeans since, in their view, governments always have funds available—had been included in the Memorandum, at America's insistence, to cover the fact that the president cannot unilaterally obligate the taxpayers' money. The Congress must first agree.

Apel spoke next. He could sign the Memorandum that day, he informed Brown, even though Germany's Minister of Finance thought otherwise. Apel, a former finance minister, knew how to handle his successor's objections. However, he added, the Bundestag had attached some conditions to Germany's participation he thought should be passed along for the record. Three required concessions from the United States Government: waiver of certain administrative surcharges; waiver of any recoupment of research and development expenditures; and waiver of certain management costs.[2] In addition, all nations would have to agree to the principle of common financing for support activities at the main operating base.[3] German industry also would have to realize the level of industrial collaboration set out in the Memorandum as well as a reasonable share of maintenance and repair work once NATO AWACS began flying. Finally, all governments would have to participate in the program as proposed in the Multilateral Memorandum of Understanding. Brown voiced no objections to Apel's remarks, although weeks later, some wished he had.

Luns continued the poll. Hansen of Norway announced that his government had, based on cabinet approval of the program, submitted a funding request to the Storting (parliament). He was prepared to sign the Memorandum—subject to the Storting's approval—if all others would sign as well. However, his government also held several technical reservations he would add for the record.

Defense Minister Emile Krieps pledged Luxembourg's continuing support by saying he could sign the Memorandum that day. Luxembourg's unflagging support for AWACS, which some found easy to take for granted, carried an importance beyond the sums of money involved for the Grand Duchy. American defense officials, for example, could and did point with effect to Luxembourg's (and the Netherlands') financial support for the interim funding effort when the United States Congress was considering the release of restricted monies for an American share.

Danson, Canada's Minister of National Defence, cast an important—and perhaps deciding—yes vote. He had successfully approached Canada's Cabinet for funds on the same day Germany's Budget Committee approved the program. He could, therefore, sign the Memorandum with the expectation all others would. Danson obviously had managed to quell his staff's protests about the lack of time for coordinating the decision document with other governmental departments. Canada's cost share, however, would be carefully bounded by both percentage and dollar limits. Mulley felt moved to explain and justify once again Britain's Nimrod decision. He, too, noted that his staff did not have sufficient time to study the Multilateral Memorandum of Understanding. Accordingly, he added, the United Kingdom would reserve the right to modify its ground sites by a separate national effort if such an approach proved more efficient than the common effort contemplated.[4] With his reservation, Mulley had in effect agreed to almost nothing, but the psychological value of his agreeing to sign was nonetheless important, keeping intact the string of yes votes which then stood at six. His agreement also required some courage since Treasury (actually, the staff of the Chancellor of the Exchequer) had rejected the Memorandum as a dreadfully flawed document. No doubt Mulley did not relish the villain's role a second time and, besides, he believed in airborne early warning systems.

Scholten nearly broke the string of yes votes. He summarized his earlier remarks on Dutch conditions for participation and added that he could not sign with the Brunssum issue unresolved. Luns quickly interjected to note the consensus building in favor of locating the Programme Office in the Netherlands. Under that condition, Scholten nodded, he could perhaps sign the Memorandum. Few can bully the Dutch.

Ruffini, the hero of six months earlier, kept his personal string intact. Despite the economic difficulties it promised, Italy could sign the Memorandum if all but one—two at the most—would sign. Ruffini was taking a chance. Although he enjoyed cabinet support for Italy's carefully constrained share, he had written a letter to his fractious parliament seeking a sustaining vote only six days before. (Ten days was the norm.) And in one of those delightful, yet sobering, vignettes underlining the vagaries that can ravish Alliance decision making, the Italian Senate's Defense Committee subsequently sustained Ruffini's action, as much because the

Committee Chairman opposed it as because of its merit.[5]

Sogaard broke the string of yes votes. He outlined Denmark's positive but tightly constrained position, then added that he could not sign the decision document. His parliament had yet to act on a cabinet-approved recommendation. Luns interrupted to ask if he could sign subject to parliamentary approval. Sogaard hesitated, discussed the proposition briefly with his aides, and answered no. Brown then suggested Sogaard use the lunch break to consult by telephone with his authorities in Copenhagen. Perhaps the American caveat, "subject to the availability of funds," could apply to Denmark as well. Sogaard did just that. After lunch, he informed ministers he could sign.

Minister Isik spoke next. He assured the Defense Planning Committee that Turkey supported the program for both military and political reasons. However, Isik continued, he did not have any legal authority to sign the Memorandum. Furthermore, he suggested, governments' representatives to the North Atlantic Council should sign the document so as to include "another nation" in the decision. Greece, "another nation," would not rejoin the Defense Planning Committee for two more years. Luns, Apel, and Brown would have none of Isik's well-intended reasoning. Each mustered arguments why the missing nation ought not to affect Turkey's decision. Isik acceded.

Luns turned to the two remaining votes. Defense Minister J. A. Loureiro dos Santos, who a matter of weeks earlier had been serving as a lieutenant colonel in Portugal's armed forces, had evidently been moved, perhaps flattered, by Brown's personal plea for him to lead his government into the program. Portugal would agree to the program as proposed in the Memorandum. Dos Santos agreed to sign, he said, in anticipation of other allies' helping Portugal rebuild its economy.

Schuurmans, representing Belgium's caretaker government, said little save to report Belgium's qualified support for the program.[6] He later remarked privately he was surprised and chagrined that other governments had agreed to proceed without Belgium. It could be that allies understand, and are generally sympathetic toward, the difficult balancing act any Belgian government faces in dealing with a fractionated Flemish and French-speaking electorate. Belgium invariably needs more time than other allies on major (and sometimes minor) security issues. Yet, Belgium invariably finds a way to carry a share of the common defense burden. With respect to AWACS, it took two and a half years and a few more changes in government before Belgium could agree to a fair share of acquisition costs.

The vote had been relatively painless—indeed, anticlimatic—in light of the frenetic activity of recent days and the endless challenges of months past. The collection of signatures at the conclusion of the second day's session was all that remained. To say few bothered then to judge the impact of the reservations accompanying ministers'·commitments would be an understatement. Euphoria may have masked reason in most quarters, but the few most responsible for the success of the initiative harbored no illusions. The ministers' reservations, and the future management problems they portended, represented a necessary condition for a major success story.

December 6th

Luns reopened the discussion on AWACS to review briefly the Brussels-Brunssum issue. Scholten announced he could join his colleagues in signing the Memorandum on the understanding that defense ministers generally agreed to locate the Programme Office in the Netherlands. Belgium's Schuurmans placed a reservation on Scholten's condition before Luns returned to the remaining agenda topics.

As Luns raised his gavel to close the meeting, he invited defense ministers to the head of the table for a signing ceremony. Each minister signed twenty-four pieces of paper, an original copy for each signatory and one for the Programme Office to hold centrally. Each original would consist of two copies: one in English, the other in French.

Only one of the eleven defense ministers present, Krieps of Luxembourg, signed without any qualifying conditions whatsoever. (The United States had managed to include its qualifying condition in the text of the document.) Brown's signature, though, meant little in financial terms without congressional action. Denmark, Italy, Norway, Portugal, and Turkey enjoyed the protection of restrictive footnotes on the cost-sharing arrangements delineated in the Memorandum. The defense ministers footnoted their signatures and added written codicils.[7] These qualifying conditions warrant illumination because they suggest how individual member's valid political requirements, when taken together, unintentionally worked counter to the larger purpose they were undertaking.

Canada

Danson carefully protected his government's position by adding four restrictions to Canada's participation in the program. Canada, of course, had long stated its requirement for all NATO nations to share program expenses.

Canada's first restriction limited its acquisition cost share in both percentage and absolute terms. By limiting its percentage share to the level (9.8 percent) proposed in the Multilateral Memorandum of Understanding, it in effect announced it would not share any acquisition funding shortfalls created by another government's decision not to participate. Canada also limited its absolute share to US $180 million (at June 1977 values). This restriction meant Canada would pay a fair share of inflation costs, but almost nothing toward real cost growth in the program. Real cost growth pressures would have to be controlled either by close management of resources or by deleting items in the program. Danson's second written restriction limited Canada's share of recurring costs for operation and support of the eighteen aircraft. The language and intent of this was almost identical to the first restriction on acquisition costs. Canada would pay no more than 9.3 percent or US $9.5 million toward annual operations and support.

The third restriction read "that a part of the Canadian contribution to the operation and support costs of the NATO AEW (airborne early warning) System be provided through participation in the military manning of the headquarters and the airborne component of the System to a level not to exceed 160 military man-years." The meaning was quite clear. That cost of 160 military man-years would be included in Canada's annual contribution of US $9.5 million toward operation and support costs. Canada's defense staff work was, as usual, a step ahead of others. They knew the Programme Office's estimate of annual recurring costs assumed governments would follow the standard NATO practice of contributing military manpower free of charge. Canada apparently knew, or at least suspected that, some governments might subsequently attack that assumption, particularly since nations would be reimbursed for their military manpower contributions. If the program reimbursed governments for one activity, why not all AWACS activities, they asked? Canada was right in protecting its position. In due course, some governments did insist on being reimbursed for their military manpower contributions to the NATO AWACS force and headquarters elements, an issue yet to be resolved.

Danson's final condition served to codify an explicit assumption used in the cost-sharing agreement. To justify Canada's major cost share (some $60 million greater than the sum that would result if Canada's normal percentage share of commonly funded budgets were applied to AWACS), Canadian industry would have to receive industrial collaboration contracts valued at $60 million.

In sum, Canada added conditions to its participation in the program to parallel those Canadian defense officials knew other governments would add. Theirs was a prudent move reflecting sound staff work and political savvy.

Denmark

Sogaard qualified his signature on the Memorandum with two written conditions.

First, the Finance Committee of the Danish Parliament would have to approve the sums involved, a technical reservation designed to comply with Danish law. Denmark's cabinet had already approved participation in the program, but, under normal circumstances, cannot obligate funds.

Sogaard's second reservation limited Denmark's financial contribution to the program. Denmark would pay a fair share of inflation costs, but nothing toward either real cost growth or funding shortages caused by any other government's non-participation. The restriction applied to acquisition costs as well as annual operations and support costs. Moreover, Sogaard added, Denmark could offer no payments until 1980, and even those would be small ones. Actually, his remarks were more forthcoming than the footnote placed on the agreement by Denmark's financial negotiator. The negotiator reserved Denmark's right to withhold payments for AWACS until 1982 by which time the great expense of acquiring F-16 fighter aircraft would have been largely met. In due course, Denmark confirmed that its payments would begin in 1982.

Germany

Apel's codicil reflected the concerns of three different elements of the German government.

To satisfy Bundestag demands, he included, by reference to his remarks of the preceding day, the condition that the United States would have to waive the surcharges discussed earlier in this chapter. The promise of these waivers was a selling point to the Bundestag committees involved in program approval. The committees decided either without prompting, or were asked by the Ministry of Defense, to ensure the promise would be kept. With scars from the main battle tank competition not yet healed, one can understand the skepticism suggested by this restriction.

The first reservation also formally incorporated Apel's remarks offered a day earlier, and discussed in a previous endnote, on the sharing of base support costs and German industrial involvement in maintenance activities. Although the Bundestag included both these conditions in its resolution approving German participation in the program, it is virtually certain some clever German staff officer maneuvered to have the Bundestag do that.

Apel's second proviso concealed more than it revealed. It read: "The Memorandum of Understanding is under review within the Federal Government because it was not received before the end of November; it must therefore be possible to make certain modifications, including an agreed solution for the problem of inflation." At first glance, this proviso seemed merely to make the point that the Ministry of Defence had not completed inter-departmental staffing of the Memorandum. And it must be possible, therefore, to amend the document. Subsequently, some Germans would argue that the statement, in effect, stipulated their share of inflation costs. This particular issue, discussed in greater detail later, would drag on for more than two years without resolution. It is highly likely that elements within the Federal Ministry of Defense—specifically within the comptroller's office—wanted this reservation appended to Apel's signature. Certainly no evidence exists to suggest the Bundestag required such a reservation.

Apel's third proviso on cost-share limits included the phrase, "my signature is based on the expectation that (Germany's share will be maintained at 30.71 percent) ...," which would appear to leave the door open for an increase in Germany's share. Open door language or not, Apel's reservation—and, indeed, all ministers' reservations—could be removed instantly or treated forever as an unqualified caveat. To date, acquisition program managers have treated these as legally binding conditions rather than as the political statements they actually are. In any event, Apel added the reservation as a warning Germany would share neither cost overruns nor some other non-participating government's share. It, like Canada's and Denmark's reservations, made the point indirectly that the AWACS program, as proposed in the Memorandum, would have to be an Alliance-wide one. Schmidt and the Federal Security Council had, of course, insisted on this point.

Apel's final reservation read, "we shall not be able to make any payments before 1979." This served to satisfy a technical objection from Germany's Minister of Finance. The Bundestag's approval of Germany's participation was tied to Germany's 1979 Fiscal Year budget, which started on 1 January. Finance Minister Matthoeffer asserted that no financial commitments could be undertaken before its effective date.

The Netherlands

Scholten acted quite generously in the three conditions he appended to participation by the Netherlands.

His first stipulation was the only one with any teeth to it. "I am willing to sign the Memorandum now ...," he wrote, "under the understanding that we have reached general agreement in the DPC that NAPMA will be located in Brunssum." He had managed to portray the Programme Office's location as a non-negotiable requirement in his oral statements, but phrased the written condition in a manner that permitted the program to go forward with the issue still technically unresolved. Belgium's Ambassador Schuurmans predictably placed a reservation on Scholten's condition.

The Dutch played Belgium's reservation cleverly, too. After ministers approved the program, the Programme Management Agency, in expanding rapidly from 40 or so people toward the nearly 200 people authorized, outgrew the temporary offices it occupied in the NATO Headquarters building just northeast of Brussels. The Netherlands waited patiently until the pressures of limited office space and family turbulence (resulting from the uncertainty of housing) built to a head, then offered the Brunssum facility as a "temporary" location until the issue of a final location could be resolved. Using the principle of unanimity, the Dutch could, of course, block any other "temporary" location, such as an office building in the Brussels area. The Belgians soon found themselves in a most difficult position. They could not yet join the program as a full participant, and, being a sensitive people, they did not wish to be responsible for the poor conditions suffered by Programme Office officials and their families. Without ceremony, Belgium removed its reservation and "permitted" the Programme Office to move to Brunssum.

Scholten did not press his second reservation concerning the question of common funding for noise abatement measures in South Limburg. He left the matter to AWACS program officials rather than to the Council. Nearly three years later, program officials agreed to provide common funding.

As for cost-share constraints, Scholten said in his third reservation that the Dutch would share real cost growth and perhaps funding shortfalls if all other participating nations would do likewise.

Norway

Hansen's written reservations were relatively long, but comparatively harmless. He did not need to restrict Norway's cost share because their financial negotiator already had, in a footnote to the payments schedule. Norway, the negotiator formally noted, could contribute nothing to acquisition costs until 1984. (In April 1981, Norway's Permanent Representative to the Council removed this restriction when it appeared the program would be in serious financial trouble.)

Other than a first proviso that the Norwegian parliament would have to ratify participation, Hansen's conditions for program approval all centered on Norway's political need to control the operation of AWACS in and around their airspace. This need was, of course, shaped by Norway's acute awareness of its common border with the Soviet Union as well as its need to keep tensions at a low level.

Turkey

Isik appended four conditions to his signature on the Multilateral Memorandum of Understanding.

The first condition reflected the fact that Turkish authorities had not yet formally addressed the proposition of participating in the program—understandably so, given the myriad problems besetting Turkey at the time. Turkey's participation, Isik simply noted, needed to be approved by "appropriate national authorities."

Isik's second and third reservations paralleled Norway's requirements to control AWACS operations in and around national airspace. The reasons were partly the same. Turkey shares a common border with Bulgaria and the Soviet Union. It also shares a border with Greece, which was the second part of the reason Isik needed to have a say about AWACS operations in the Aegean region. Overflight rights and associated issues had been resolved either in the text of, or by footnote to, the Memorandum, thanks to Walsh's intercession with the Greeks and Turks. Isik's reservation served as an insurance policy.

Turkey's fourth reservation called for an AWACS forward operation base to be established in Turkey. The reservation was welcomed because a base in Turkey offered important military advantages to the Alliance.

Greece

On 22 December 1978, Assistant Secretary General Walsh signed a covering memorandum to NATO's Permanent Representatives, notifying governments that all parties had signed a supplement to the Memorandum admitting Greece as a full participant in the program. Not surprisingly, the Greek Ambassador to NATO appended a list of conditions to his signature.

Greece chose to limit its financial participation in both the acquisition and operation phases to the sums delineated in the Memorandum. This amounted to a concession since Greece had argued during the negotiating sessions for AWACS cost-shares to be adjusted to account for each government's defense expenditures, as measured by the percentage of the national product devoted to defense. The Greek representative got nowhere with the argument, probably because only three nations (Greece, Turkey, and the United States) would have enjoyed reduced shares.

Greece's second condition, the right to approve operations in and over its territory, served as its insurance policy on AWACS flights over the southeast flank of NATO Europe.

Finally, the Ambassador stipulated that a forward operating base had to be established in Greece. In military terms, forward bases in both Greece and Turkey might not be absolutely necessary, particularly in light of the limited funds available. In political terms, however, the need for those in both countries was indisputable.

After more than two years of fairly intense negotiations and more than a few political compromises, defense ministers had at last approved the program. Contrary to expectations in some quarters, however, the ministers' approval did not mark the end of important political decisions or compromises on NATO AWACS. It marked the beginning. Since they were political choices—although often raised in the guise of management choices—they too were influenced by the quirks and imperatives of coalition and national politics.

6. AN IMPERFECT AGREEMENT?

Two days after defense ministers signed the Memorandum, the North Atlantic Council, meeting in ministerial session, unanimously approved a Charter establishing the management organization for AWACS as a legal NATO entity.[1] The organization consisted of two elements: a policy-setting Board of Directors comprised of one senior representative from each participating government; and a subordinate Programme Management Agency to implement the acquisition effort.

Unlike the Multilateral Memorandum of Understanding, which included great—indeed, one could argue, excessive—detail, the Charter stood with few exceptions as a model of generalities. It in effect invited the Board to define the limits of its authority in meeting its responsibilities. Charter language notwithstanding, two realities quickly circumscribed the practical limits of the Board's authority.

The Board could move no further or faster on resolving policy issues (that is to say, political issues) than the most myopic or strong-willed member would permit. Some of the specialists who framed the Charter, perhaps recognizing that the principle of unanimity invariably leads to lowest common denominator solutions, had toyed with the notion of weighted votes.[2] They quickly (and correctly) rejected the notion for practical and political reasons. The Board would thus remain a microcosm of the North Atlantic Alliance.

In implementing the ministers' decision, the Board was handicapped no more by common denominator politics, however, than by the financial constraints sprinkled throughout the Memorandum in the name of political accommodation. The amounts and phasing of cost shares had been firmly established by ministerial decree. Initial cost estimates—intended only to give governments some reasonably accurate sense of AWACS' affordability—had in effect become cost ceilings. And the staggered payments compromise—designed to balance incremental funding requirements with governments' future budget commitments—had become a rigid timetable. Thus, the Board and all other parties involved in acquiring the program would simply have to push, pry, and squeeze AWACS under the ceiling and into a set funding schedule. It was not simple, however.

A First Test

The first test came by way of the Acquisition Agreement. This document, to be signed by the "customer" (the Programme Management Agency acting on behalf of governments) and his "agent" (the United States Air Force acting on behalf of the American Government), set out the terms and conditions of the customer-agent relationship. It also set out the Air Force's detailed estimates of costs and schedules for the airborne component of the program. Those quite obviously were only as accurate as the pricing information provided by dozens of commercial and government sources. And this information, in turn, was sensitive to pricing assumptions.

Therein lay the principal source of misunderstandings and, in time, irritation over cost growth pressures. There was another source as well. The cost data, on which ministers based their decision and set ceilings, rested on quicksand. Delay after delay to accommodate political needs in capitals had invalidated the time limits, and thus the accuracy, of the estimates. To be sure, the cost data were revalidated prior to the December meeting of defense ministers, but the results were apparently more form than substance. It takes time and money to revise cost estimates, and both were in short supply during the months prior to the Defense Planning Committee meeting. Moreover, some subcontractors declined to confirm or rebid prices because they doubted AWACS would ever fly. Best estimates had to suffice.

But, they did not. Some prices had risen faster than estimated inflation rates. A few items had been priced incorrectly or incompletely, acquisition lead times had stretched, and the Programme Office had added items.[3] Taken together, they exerted tremendous upward pressure on aircraft acquisition costs. The United States Air Force attempted to provide some relief by changing production assumptions. By assuming another six American AWACS would be funded by the Congress, the upward cost pressures for NATO's program could be partially capped, and one could worry later about the difficulty of justifying the need for two AWACS programs.[4] The Air Force quietly incorporated the change in the draft Acquisition Agreement, staffed it through the Office of the Secretary of Defense, and passed it to Europe for review.

Shah Mohammed Reza Pahlavi's Iranian government, which had ordered seven AWACS, fell on 17 January 1979. Several weeks later, Iran's new government cancelled the Shah's AWACS order. Those same seven AWACS would have provided important cost savings to the NATO program.

Confusion. Capitals inquired about the cost impact to NATO. Negligible, whispered the prime contractor.[5] Maybe $35 million, said the Department of Defense in carefully chosen words. Truth, in this instance, depended on assumptions. The prime contractor based cost estimates for ministers' consideration on twenty-five American, seven Iranian, and eighteen NATO AWACS. By adding six more American aircraft, as the Department of Defense had done in the latest draft of the Acquisition Agreement, and subtracting seven Iranian aircraft, the cost effect to customers would be negligible. By contrast, the Department of Defense based its draft Acquisition Agreement cost estimates on thirty-one American, seven Iranian, and eighteen NATO AWACS. It had of course already applied the cost benefits to NATO from the additional six American AWACS and thus could not offset the loss of the Iranian program. In due course, but after feelings had been bruised, European defense establishments accepted the Department's explanation of the affair.

The cost-share constraints decreed by several governments via footnote and codicil had perhaps served a contrary purpose. Possibly, those governments did intend to accept a lesser program as long as their shares held constant but, more likely, however, they intended to send warning signals to two camps. There would be no "free rides" on the AWACS program, said some governments, stating that they would not increase their shares to cover funding shortfalls from others not participating. National treasuries would not be opened to sponsor the outrageous cost overruns for which defense industries are sometimes famous.

Intentions aside, political difficulties—much more than financial difficulties—limited the prospects for change in the cost-sharing agreement. Proportionate increases, for example, would require the unanimous consent of participating governments. Securing unanimous agreement on any controversial initiative, particularly one affecting national treasuries, is, almost by definition, a trying, time-consuming proposition. Who would have been willing to undertake such an effort only a few months after the program started?

The United States, for political reasons, never considered it. American defense officials had assured the Allies, when the issue of affordability occupied center stage, of the low probability for cost growth in a mature production program like AWACS. The potential for charges of perfidy signalled caution. Then, too, American participation in the program was, at that moment, under review by the Congress. Asking for additional monies before the Congress approved the first year's funding increment—and, in practical terms, the entire program with its millions in cost waivers and exceptions to public law—would have been a politically clumsy move.

Thus, the first test set a pattern for future cost problems. Cost-growth pressures, no matter the source, could be ameliorated only by increasingly painful reductions in military capability. The political need for cost constraints curtailed all other program management options, and each subsequent cut would necessarily slash increasingly deeper as managers deleted items already in production.

The Staggered Payments Schedule

The staggered payments schedule posed management problems just as severe as those posed by the politically mandated cost ceilings. In many procurement programs, spending money faster can often reduce final prices, but, in any event, not spending money at the rate needed to support efficient production always increases the final price. Acquisition managers faced the worst of it from two directions. They could neither exceed the cost ceiling nor speed payments to reduce cost growth pressures.

Time and circumstances had eroded the already tenuous viability of the original compromise on national payments. To begin with, the sum of the nations' annual payments did not match annual funding requirements even with the compromise, although no government quarreled with their right and need to do so. Italy's qualified participation, as well as the footnotes of Denmark and Norway to the payments schedule, promised a substantial shortage of funds by 1983. Belgium's inability (until mid-1981) to agree to an acquisition share compounded the problem. Even without these politically induced funding shortages, other events seemed to conspire against the NATO program.

Ministers approved the program six months later than the starting date assumed in the payments profile and then did not meet the interim funding

AN IMPERFECT AGREEMENT? 149

levels needed fully to protect costs and schedules. The United States would not procure its six additional AWACS at the same rate planned for Iran's cancelled program. Then, too, competition, and thus acquisition lead times, increased for the items common to most other aircraft. Airlines ordered more new airplanes to meet the boom in deregulated air travel and take advantage of a new generation of fuel-efficient commercial aircraft just as the production capacity of fewer suppliers bottomed out. NATO AWACS was trapped in a seller's market. And the Board of Directors was trapped with almost no flexibility to deal with changed circumstances not of its own doing.

The staggered payments schedule sired another problem that led to a hand-wringing exercise in at least two capitals and a hand-washing exercise in another. Governments had agreed from the outset of negotiations to adjust their agreed cost shares for the effects of inflation. Even without staggered payments, the accounting problem would have been monumental, but manageable.[6] With staggered payments, political sophistry entered the equation.

Governments handed the problem to the Federal Republic of Germany and the United States to solve. Not only were they funding well over 70 percent of program costs, the bulk of their respective payments stood at opposite ends of the seven-year acquisition effort. Unfortunately, their respective views of inflation adjustments also stood poles apart.

The United States and others proposed that annual payments, whenever nations rendered them, be adjusted to maintain constant purchasing power. Estimated acquisition costs in the Multilateral Memorandum of Understanding agreed and capped by

150 AN IMPERFECT AGREEMENT?

defense ministers were expressed in June 1977 US dollars. If these relative financial burdens as expressed in cost-share percentages were to be preserved—a point insisted on by all governments—their annual payments necessarily were expressed in June 1977 US dollars as well. Logically, annual payments delineated in the Memorandum would have to be adjusted to maintain the purchasing power of base year dollars.

Germany insisted also that it had bargained to pay only its agreed base year annual payment as detailed in the Memorandum, plus a fair share of annual inflation—a fair share being defined as its agreed percentage share (30.71 percent) of program costs. Since Germany's annual base year percentage share ranged from a low of 15 to 20 percent in the early years to a high of nearly 70 percent in the late years, its inflation sharing method would have, over time, shifted relative financial burdens to the advantage of late-paying governments. German defense officials did not dispute that conclusion. In fact, some argued that had always been the point of their inflation sharing plan.

The issue dragged on for more than two years. Canada, an early-paying nation like the United States, attempted to discuss the problem with Germany, encountered intransigence—a political stance not uncommon among governments in the NATO AWACS program—and invited America to carry on. The United States asked Germany to accelerate its annual base year payments, which, in effect, would render the inflation issue moot. Germany countered with its own compromise proposal to split the difference. In due course, all other governments voted for the constant purchasing power approach wanted by the United States and Canada.[7] As of this writing, Germany appears to be moving toward approving the otherwise unanimous approach. It has, in any event, already agreed to adjust its annual payments to maintain constant purchasing power without prejudice to a final resolution.

Fiscal logic aside, Germany possessed a decent political argument for its inflation sharing method, since the Memorandum remained vague on the subject of inflation because of its reservations. For similar reasons, the payment schedule in the Memorandum did not specify constant year currencies, even if a different article in the document established program costs in 1977 dollars and the totals in the payments schedule equalled total program costs in 1977 dollars. Apel's reservation to the Memorandum reflected a well-known German concern and perhaps even a position, although one could argue its meaning as written.

Theories and facts on why the Federal Republic resisted accepting a demonstrably equitable inflation sharing method are less relevant than the fact that governments, knowing of loose ends and escape hatches, agreed to a staggered payments schedule. It stood as one of two political compromises in the program where good intentions overruled good sense. Good intentions, as one wag declared, tend to randomize the workability of agreements.

Termination Liability

The termination liability issue and its ramifications perhaps demonstrate another feature of protracted negotiations: decisions taken incrementally can convolute final agreements.

Incremental decisions in this case occurred over a nearly two-year period at intervals sufficiently long for people not to challenge earlier decisions. In early 1977, the United States Department of Defense agreed to waive prepayment of termination liability—to ease cash flow needs early in the program—when it seemed the program would be a more-or-less normal Foreign Military Sale.[8] Subsequently, the Department acceded to the allies' strongly expressed wishes to treat AWACS as a cooperative acquisition program rather than a Foreign Military Sale. A few months later, the allies endorsed a "loophole" acquisition arrangement devised by the Pentagon that largely removed the sale of AWACS from Foreign Military Sales procedures and surcharges.[9] Finally, about eight months later, the allies persuaded the Department to seek congressional waiver of the remaining surcharges.

Had the Pentagon agreed from the outset to seek congressional waiver of certain objectionable Foreign Military Sale procedures and surcharges, the program probably would have remained just that.[10] Under those circumstances, termination liability coverage would not have become an issue between the contractor and program managers because the United States Government would have been the party contracting for the eighteen airplanes.

From the prime contractor's point of view, the acquisition arrangements did not include adequate guarantees for the financial liabilities normally incurred during a billion dollar plus production program. Those liabilities, consisting principally of either non-cancellable commitments to suppliers or production cutback costs amounted to $200 to $300 million at their highest point. If NATO terminated the program—and circumstances of the political agreement between governments suggested a possibility of termination at any time for any number of reasons—the prime contractor enjoyed little legal recourse. Which party could be sued, if it came to that, for termination costs? The Programme Management Agency? The contracting party for the eighteen airplanes? It held no assets except those provided in installments by governments and, moreover, it enjoyed immunity from litigation. Could the governments be sued? Only at their pleasure. Of course, governments would stand by their commitments, but under some circumstances it might take months of negotiation to sort out the extent of liabilities and the sharing of them.

In the meantime and before then, because the liabilities were unsecured, creditors would consider them as a potential debit affecting the contractor's credit rating. That, in turn, would raise the cost of borrowing and consequently the cost of the program. Certainly, one can reasonably conclude that the contractor may have been justified in seeking both a higher profit margin because of the greater risk and some better guarantee for the unsecured liabilities.

The Department of Defense tried to mitigate the problem by seeking congressional authorization for an American share of termination liability costs. That helped some, but not enough. Any commercial credit guarantees for the balance would cost money governments already said they could not afford. From the allies point of view, political commitments from defense ministers were as binding as any contract. Eventually the contractor reluctantly agreed, and a spokesperson vowed they would never enter into an agreement again where political commitments served as collateral for a billion-plus dollar contract. Fortunately for NATO, there is an important element of statesmanship in large companies like Boeing Aerospace, the prime contractor for AWACS.

This vignette on liabilities illustrates other points beyond the pitfalls of incremental decision making. Goodwill and political commitments between governments do not easily translate into enforceable "legal" agreements on the basis of which least-cost contracts can be negotiated. The termination liability problem represented, like others stemming from the staggered payments schedule, another instance where attempts to control spending may have led to added costs.

An Imperfect Agreement?

The NATO AWACS agreement is a remarkable political achievement—remarkable by definition since NATO in its thirty-year history had never undertaken a similar initiative. As a legally binding acquisition agreement, however, it is less than remarkable. Paradoxically, a few of the accommodations leading to, and indeed necessary for, the political achievement resulted in the troublesome flaws plaguing those charged with executing the agreement.

Consider initially the two most important political accommodations and their impacts.

First, all governments at one time or another had to wait for others to prepare for and complete internal decision-making processes. Apel's detailed, careful preparation for parliamentary approval, for example, consumed six months which led to two extensions of the interim funding effort. Yet, also for political reasons, Germany could not contribute to that effort which, among other reasons in other capitals—all politically motivated—resulted in the interim effort's being underfunded. The underfunded effort, in turn, contributed to cost growth pressures. Indeed, delay by itself contributed to those pressures. And of course, for political reasons, Germany joined a number of other governments in capping cost shares. America's time-consuming and adversarial political process, to cite another of many examples, contributed to Apel's political problems as well as to program funding problems. The Congress said it would not consider American participation in the program until other governments agreed to acquire AWACS. Consequently, the United States could not cover its share of funding in 1979—after the program started—until the Congress passed, and the President signed into law, a defense budget supplemental. The resulting slow start may or may not have increased acquisition costs, but it certainly foreclosed the opportunity possibly to reduce cost growth pressures by a faster production start.

Second, all governments accepted without serious challenge all other governments' declared needs—principally political in origin—for cost shares constrained in timing and amount. This particular accommodation stands largely responsible for the lack of flexibility suffered by acquisition managers. It also led directly to the inflation adjustment issue and indirectly to the termination liability issue.

On the other hand, many other political accommodations—some between governments and some within governments—did not impinge directly on implementation of the program. But they affected attitudes which, one could argue, did create management difficulties for the program. Included in this category would be, among others: linkages between NATO AWACS and other cooperative programs; reordering of defense budgets to make room for an AWACS share; bending national priorities to suit Alliance needs; and waiving, or otherwise making exceptions to, national laws, policies, and procedures. There is a not-too-obvious theme common to each of these. Very senior officials in Allied governments agreed to the accommodation over the protests of staffs and minority elements in legislatures or cabinets. Many of the aggrieved parties exacted petty retribution while some minority elements insisted on hamstringing conditions. Other staffs pouted.

Still, there clearly would have been no NATO AWACS program without political compromise, most of which worked so well that few can remember the details, much less the stir they created when governments first proposed them. The few that created subsequent management problems in the acquisition program seemed a small price to pay for such a bold, unprecedented venture.

Imperfections and unimaginative bureaucrats, indeed, fade to insignificance in the larger context of what AWACS means to NATO. Critics of the agreement need to be reminded of first principles. AWACS will correct a glaring deficiency in NATO's air defense posture and, by extension, its deterrent posture. As a bonus, it will also multiply the effectiveness of NATO's entire air defense network. (The day will come, one suspects, when governments will wish they had acquired a larger AWACS force.) And as the final, most important point, AWACS demonstrates that visionaries still man the helm of the North Atlantic Alliance.

AUTHOR'S EPILOGUE

I owe a special thanks to Dr. Larry Legere, Defense Advisor, United States Mission to NATO, for unblocking the circumstances that delayed publication of this book for a number of years. Fortunately, the passage of time has not significantly eroded the accuracy and relevance of the accounts detailed in the preceding chapters. Indeed, the delay, because it spurs a need for an explanatory postscript, may be fortuitous insofar as it allows the opportunity to report in brief detail how wildly—and, to some, unexpectedly—successful the NATO AWACS initiative proved to be. And that success underscores the relevance, to the choices facing NATO today, of the process of political compromise examined in this book.

The proof of success did not begin to emerge, however, until nearly three years after Ministers approved the program. It took that long for the financial, budgetary, and political aftermath of "the imperfect agreement" (treated in Chapter 6) to recede. Said another way, it took that long—to cite a few principal examples of many—for Belgium to commit to a full acquisition share, for Germany to agree to inflate its annual payments to maintain constant purchasing power, and for Italy formally to propose a payments schedule for the last three-quarters of its acquisition cost-share. It also may have very well taken that long for the Programme Management Agency and most members of the Board of Directors, individually and collectively, to pull together toward common objectives.

Which of the two—a favorable coalescence of related, yet independent, events, or a coalescence of the program's management structure—accounts more for the success of NATO AWACS cannot be argued decisively. The answer, which one suspects is unequal bits of both, may not matter. Today's wisdom in NATO—among those embarked on other collective security initiatives who look to the AWACS program for constructive clues—holds that the management structure's autonomy (and competence) accounts more than any other single factor for NATO AWACS' success. To be sure, the Board of Directors' autonomy, particularly in matters of budget and finance, stands without precedence among NATO Procurement and Logistics Organizations. Why that is so, and why it matters, warrants a fuller explanation.

The Board did not assume such autonomy; the North Atlantic Council conferred it in the Charter previously cited and subsequently confirmed it in unambiguous language. At the high point of cost and budget pressures in 1980, the Board judged the funds available would prove insufficient to acquire the approved program. Unable, or perhaps unwilling, to resolve the dilemma, it formally sought the Council's guidance. The Council said, in effect, the choice is yours within the funds available; delete what you must, but delete airplanes only as a last resort.

What followed is more important in thrust than in detail. The Board preserved aircraft by cutting

AUTHOR'S EPILOGUE 161

deeply, albeit temporarily as it happened, into system capabilities. Far more significantly, it seemed to accept that, thenceforth, there would be no outside help in resolving seemingly intractable problems. Over the next few years, the Board thus took any number of decisions that bumped up against, and occasionally moved well past, NATO's normal way of doing business. The smiles conferred on the successes that followed outnumbered, if not overwhelmed, the raised eyebrows and occasional frowns of disapproval as the Board countenanced a rather unique set of financial regulations, arranged to register the aircraft in Luxembourg, used program-generated income to restore previously deferred or deleted system capabilities, unilaterally extended its tenure several years, and generally built a first-class NATO air force. One is sorely tempted, if NATO AWACS be a valid precedent, to argue that autonomy in budget matters and managerial competence stand as the essential ingredients for success in collective security initiatives.

During the same period, virtually all other parties involved in the program generally matched the foregoing standards of achievement. Contractors for the aircraft and its systems delivered all eighteen units well ahead of schedule (by months) and substantially under the contracted cost-ceiling (by tens of millions of dollars). NATO's military structure adjusted and expanded to command and control with precious few hiccups, the new—and first—NATO air force. Governments' military establishments assigned their very finest and most experienced people to fill aircrew, staff, and support requirements. Multinational aircrews proved to be no major problem as the NATO force of AWACS

AUTHOR'S EPILOGUE

equalled, and often exceeded, the very high standards of readiness and achievement registered by the US AWACS force. Success seemed to beget success.

But there were problems—and solutions that pleased almost no one.

The modifications to NATO's air defense ground environment, necessary for the new aircraft and existing air defense network to work together as a team, proved far more complex politically and programmatically than anyone had imagined. And such complexities always create cost pressures. Politically, governments could agree in principle to reduce the number of modified ground sites (to reduce costs), but found it exceptionally difficult to agree to specifics, particularly when the specifics involved a site or sites in their territory. Programmatically, the major differences in site configurations, and the attendant need for customized engineering and software solutions, consumed 50 percent more time and money than had been allocated to the effort. Over time, the Management Agency and the Board found solutions and money for the modification effort. And although the search for both created strains and, at times, eroded goodwill among coalition partners, the success of it stands clearly as the greatest achievement in the management of a unique program.

Negotiating the arrangements for depot level maintenance, on the other hand, proved a heartbreak. Depot level maintenance, requiring expensive equipment and facilities for major system modifications, overhauls, and the like, would yield important economic benefits: $80 million in capital investment and another $12 million in recurring annual costs. Moreover, the work to be done, and the equipment needed for that work, were relatively advanced technologically and thus attractive to certain governments looking to gain or maintain a competitive position in the aerospace marketplace. Whether for these likely reasons, the love of challenge by some Board members, or hidden reasons such as behind-the-scene commitments, negotiations over depot level maintenance nearly matched the intensity and duration of negotiations needed to put the entire program together several years earlier.

Indeed, this episode by itself may deserve a fuller discussion and analysis than is appropriate in an epilogue, or, for that matter, in a book focused on political compromise in NATO. Compromise implies a range of choices. As it turned out, the only choices realistically available to the Board were to accept or reject a flawed depot level maintenance arrangement. They accepted the flaws in the interest of preserving the larger, nobler successes of the program.

The arrangements called for a sole-source contract that included assurances, bordering on guarantees, of economic offsets or workshares for designated firms in every nation participating in the program, except in the United States. Lest this seem unfair to the Americans, one must immediately add that many of the spares and some, perhaps much, of the equipment could be acquired only from American vendors. If everyone received a slice of the pie, what flaws could exist? Well, the process and circumstances of negotiations were flawed because the many had to accommodate unexplained agreements reached in private by the few. The outcome was flawed because it violated the "least-cost" standards consistently upheld in earlier Board decisions. Finally, the arrangements may be flawed because the users' needs—the operators' needs—seemed curiously less important than other considerations. Such, occasionally, is the price of unanimity.

Two other major events relevant to this book occurred late in 1986. First, the United Kingdom decided, after much agonizing, to write off most of its considerable investments in the failed Nimrod airborne early warning program in favor of acquiring at least six AWACS. Shortly thereafter, France decided to acquire a national AWACS force (of three aircraft, at present). Behind each of these decisions stands, no doubt, a story with fascinating twists and turns that, alas, must await some other author for the telling. Whatever the story, the striking success of the NATO AWACS program must have played a powerful role in both governments' decisions.

This book has attempted to shed light on a narrow instance of give and take among NATO governments. But this book is not just about political process, nor just about a truly remarkable success story arising from that process. It is also, I hope, a book about people, few if any of whom consider themselves heroic, although their deeds were often heroic. It is on these worthy people, and those who follow them, that the continued good health of the North Atlantic Alliance depends. They will all, I know, acquit themselves honorably.

Arnold Lee Tessmer
1988

ENDNOTES

1. A Question of Affordability

1. Methods of expressing cost data for a given system can approach dizzying levels. Unit acquisition cost is the basic term, better known as unit "fly away" or "drive away" cost. System acquisition cost is unit acquisition cost plus the cost of an initial lay-in of system-peculiar spare parts plus engine spares. Program acquisition cost is system acquisition cost plus a pro rata share of the program's total research, development, test, and evaluation costs. Life cycle cost is program acquisition cost plus a lifetime of estimated operating and maintenance costs. These costs can be expressed individually, or in the aggregate, as then year (with estimated inflation folded in) or base-year costs. Each cost measure yields a specific meaning to those in the know, but critics and advocates alike occasionally play fast and loose with cost data for a particular program. Thus, for example, critics decried the B-1 for costing $23-25 billion (total then year program acquisition costs) while its advocates pointed to a $50 million price tag (base-year-unit-acquisition cost). The $75 million for one AWACS cited in the text is a nicely rounded number that falls somewhere in the middle of the extremes.

2. AWACS was being considered as the system to correct deficiencies in the NATO Air Defense Ground Environment, itself a collectively acquired—but nationally operated—system of air defense radar and intercept control centers. The notion of a collective acquisition effort for AWACS, therefore, was supported by both precedent and high cost. Which of these first sparked the idea of a

collective AWACS program is apparently lost to history and, in any event, not terribly important. Clearly, however, high cost sustained the idea of a collectively owned and operated AWACS force.

3. US, Congress, Senate, Senator Eagleton (D-Mo) speaking for an Amendment (No. 527) to restrict the expenditure of monies authorized and appropriated for Air Force AWACS, 94th Congress, 1st Session, 5 June 1975, *Congressional Record* 121:17387-93, included for the record an unclassified version of a General Accounting Office Report, dated 20 February 1975, "AWACS: Factors Impacting on a Production Decision." A second report (B-163058, dated March 1974) critical of AWACS during this period has not been released to the public.

4. One who would have reluctantly traded combat aircraft for AWACS was General David C. Jones, then Chief of Staff, United States Air Force. See, for example, his testimony before the Defense Subcommittee of the House Appropriations Committee on 3 February 1976. US, Congress, House of Representatives, *Hearings Before a Subcommittee of the Committee on Appropriations*, Part 1, 94th Congress, 2nd Session, 1976, pp. 118-19.

5. The Military Committee, the most senior military body in the NATO Alliance, is composed of the Chiefs of the Armed Forces from all member countries except Iceland, which fields no military forces. The Military Committee recommends initiatives and courses of action to NATO's political councils and provides guidance on military questions to the Major NATO Commanders. A priority-one requirement is, as the term suggests, an urgently needed capability.

6. The earth's curvature limits a ground-based radar's horizon to about twenty miles, the precise range depending on variables such as terrain and foliage. In practical terms, this means that low flying aircraft can often evade detection altogether, as happened, for example, when the Soviet defector, Balenko, flew his MIG 25 Foxbat under

Japanese air defense radars to land undetected at an airfield in Hokkaido. See *Newsweek* 88 (20 September 1976):63.

7. See, for example, R. James Woolsey's pan of planning assumptions in his, "Systems Analysis: The Bingo Game in the Basement of the Pentagon," *Armed Forces Journal*, Vol. 117, No. 8 (March 1980):35-36. Although overstating the intent of analysts, Woolsey nevertheless paints an accurate picture of the importance of assumptions in arriving at force structure needs.

8. Contrary to Pentagon folklore of the time, Parliament had not granted the Ministry of Defence money—£250 to £300 million was the sum commonly cited—for a Shackleton replacement. Parliament normally neither examines the merit of defense programs in detail nor appropriates funds, in the American sense of the word, budget line item by budget line item.

9. US, Congress, Senate, Committee on Armed Services, *Authorizing Appropriations for Fiscal Year 1977 for Military Procurement, Research and Development, and Active Duty, Selected Reserve, and Civilian Personnel Strengths and for Other Purposes*, Report No. 94-878, 94th Congress, 2nd Session, 1976. This report states, in part: "The Committee last year stated that it believed the United States had a current need for twenty-one to twenty-four AWACS planes in the US Air Force, including a US share of the NATO force. The committee again states this appears to be a reasonable force objective in light of the current threat, and therefore recommends approval of the six planes in the fiscal year 1977 request plus the advance procurement toward six more next year. This implies procurement of a total of twenty-five AWACS planes for the US Air Force, and at the same time will protect the option for NATO to participate in the program by 1977 without causing a production line break."

10. Read, for example, the floor debate in the United States Senate on Senator Eagleton's amendment to tie

release of Air Force AWACS production monies to an Alliance decision to acquire AWACS. *Congressional Record* 121:17385-410. On the House side, read the *Congressional Record* 121:15048-052 where Representative Schroeder (D-Colo.) attempted to delete all AWACS production monies from the House version of the Fiscal Year 1976 Defense Authorization Bill. One of the principal arguments used to defeat both of these and other attempts to terminate or delay AWACS was the promise of a NATO program. Thus, early on, it proved useful upon occasion to hold one program hostage to the other.

11. I credit the United States Air Force, because the most senior Air Force leadership (including the Chief of Staff, General David C. Jones) strongly supported AWACS and at least tacitly approved an initiative to educate NATO Allies on the merits of the airplane. General Jones established an ad hoc group, called the AWACS Task Force, for that and other tasks. The group performed admirably during its four-year existence under a series of particularly able general officers, including (then) Brigadier General John S. Pustay, (then) Lieutenant General William C. Moore, and (then) Brigadier General Richard T. Boverie. Not all elements of the Air Force shared General Jones' enthusiasm for AWACS.

12. The Defense Production Sharing Agreement calls for Canada and the United States to coordinate their economic efforts in defense acquisition programs. What it amounts to is a kind of free market arrangement for Canadian and American defense contractors, with some effort taken to keep track of the balance of defense trade. Most of the details can be found in the United States Defense Acquisition Regulations.

13. US Department of State, *Aide Memoire* delivered to the Canadian Government by the Embassy of the United States on 4 June 1976.

14. US Air Force, Assistant to the Chief of Staff for Studies and Analysis, a classified study entitled (title

unclassified), "AWACS-Alternatives and Opportunities in Air Defense," December 1975.

15. The term "minor-share" used frequently throughout this study was coined by the NATO staff to describe the cost shares, however they might be mathematically derived, of those governments whose industries would not participate in manufacturing AWACS components. These cost shares were not minor to the governments involved.

16. (Then) Brigadier General John Piotrowski, Commander of the 552nd AWACS Wing at Tinker Air Force Base, Oklahoma. The AWACS, flying at 30,000 feet—approximately its normal operating altitude—can detect, track, and vector interceptors into firing positions against aircraft flying at extremely low altitudes out to its radar horizon of well beyond 200 miles. Its capabilities against aircraft flying at higher altitudes are significantly greater. Because of its unique radar and data processing abilities, AWACS can continue to operate quite effectively when opposing forces employ electronic countermeasures. Unlike ground based radar's fragmented view of events, the AWACS "big picture" capabilities are difficult to thwart by electronic deception, feints, or saturation. Consequently, it can foreclose surprise air attacks and permit air battle commanders to allocate defense assets much more effectively.

17. The decision making machinery in this instance called for the proposal to go to the Secretary General, Joseph M. A. H. Luns, thence to governments' Permanent Representatives (ambassadors to NATO) meeting as the Defense Planning Committee in permanent session, and then to defense ministers meeting as the Defense Planning Committee in ministerial session. Permanent Representatives are two-hatted in the sense they also meet normally every week as the North Atlantic Council in permanent session, representing foreign ministers.

18. Aye votes on Senator Eagleton's and Representative Schroeder's respective amendments to hamstring AWACS

170   A QUESTION OF AFFORDABILITY

read, with some exceptions, like a roll call of liberal Democrats. See the *Congressional Record* 121:17410 and 121:15052.

19. Interview with Georg Leber, 17 March 1981, in Bonn, Federal Republic of Germany. Leber was Germany's Minister of Defense from 7 July 1972 to 16 February 1978.

20. Interview with Dr. Karl Schnell, 18 March 1981, in Baden-Baden, Federal Republic of Germany. Dr. Schnell served as State Secretary for Defense (equivalent to a Deputy Minister of Defense) from 1976 to 1980. He is now retired from government service.

21. Foot-dragging from a German point of view was thoroughness from an American point of view. Germany offered its main battle tank, Leopard II, as a candidate to meet the American Army's new main battle tank requirement. After nearly two years of rigorous testing, the Army announced it preferred the American designed tank (the XM-1). Having failed to field a common tank, which would have yielded important battlefield advantages, senior defense officials tried to salvage some semblance of common weaponry by trying to "harmonize" (their word) the two tanks' major components (engines, guns, tracks, etc.). Tank gun evaluations, scheduled for completion in January 1977, were slipped several times, thereby contributing to Germany's suspicions that elements of the Army, American industry, and the Congress would oppose procuring any major weapon system of German design.

22. Drawn from a reporting cable sent to the Departments of State and Defense on 9 December 1976 by the United States Mission to NATO Headquarters.

23. NATO Press Communique M-DPC-2(76)17, dated 8 December 1976.

24. Reconstructed from the collective memories of Allied staff officers involved in the program. The sums cited may be slightly inaccurate, but are close enough for purposes of this discussion.

25. Allies and elements of the Congress held opposing views on at least one aspect of business arrangements. Allies generally thought the surcharges levied on arms sales inappropriate for AWACS. Some members of Congress were particularly concerned at the prospect NATO might pay less for AWACS than the United States—the difference being viewed as a "subsidy." See the *Congressional Record* 121:6684-5.

26. This component, called Government Furnished Equipment, comprises those items the government buys in bulk quantities (radios, for example) at a lower price than a small-order customer could possibly match or those services not available from a commercial vendor (training of air crews, for example). It accounted for well more than $300 million in the NATO AWACS cost estimate.

27. Section 21 Public Law 94-329 (International Security Assistance and Arms Export Control Act of 1976; H.R. 13680) 90 Stat. 729, approved 30 June 1976. This Act consolidated and revised previous legislation relating to reimbursable military exports. The Act has been amended several times since.

28. US, Congress, Senate, 95th Congress, 1st Session, Hearings before the Committee on Armed Services on *Fiscal Year 1978 Authorization for Military Procurement, Research and Development, and Active Duty, Selected Reserve, and Civilian Personnel Strengths*, Part 6, Tactical Air, 2, 3, 4, 7, 8 March 1977, pp. 4477-4481. Dr. Currie cited the range 25 to 33 percent in a letter to the Congress, but used other figures (25 to 30 percent, for example) in verbal testimony. The reference cited here captures a dialogue between Dr. Parker (Currie's successor) and the Committee on Armed Services where the contradiction was laid to rest. The Committee's negative reaction to a 33 percent share came to serve as a guideline for American negotiators.

29. The arithmetic here, reflecting the national cost of AWACS cited earlier in Chapter 1, is less important than

the argument. The upper limits of the American cost-share were constrained by the economic choice described.

30. Normal procedures in a Foreign Military Sale require the "customer" (another government) to establish an escrow account to cover the cost of premature termination of contracts for the equipment being purchased. The escrow account builds during the early stages of the contract period, when the manufacturer's liabilities are greatest, then dwindles toward zero as the last item comes off the production line. The sale price is not affected by this arrangement, but cash flow is.

31. The $125 million in surcharges comprised about $65 million in research and development surcharges (based on a 4 percent recoupment of the Air Force's investment); $45 million in administrative surcharges; and $15 million in asset use and rental charges (for the use of government-owned facilities and equipment).

32. The General Accounting Office retains the right to audit any time congressionally appropriated monies are involved, as they may have been in European industries' production of AWACS components.

33. Interview with Georg Leber, 17 March 1981. Leber said Padberg held instructions for a ceiling on a percentage cost-share he could have accepted ad referendum. Leber understandably did not recall the ceiling, but did say it was tied to the number of other participants. (Rumors of the day placed the ceiling at about 20 to 22 percent.)

34. Interview with Dale Babione, 25 February 1981, in Washington, DC. Babione did not recall the exact amounts.

35. Production of AWACS components in Europe and Canada would incur cost penalties because of the capital investment needed for tools, jigs, technical data packages, and so forth. Recurring costs would also be higher for a time (perhaps always depending on comparative wage

scales) because of what is referred to as "learning curve" penalties. Workers are more efficient the twentieth time they do something than they are the first time. Inefficiency costs money.

2. The Nimrod Decision

1. Based on interviews with the Honourable Frederick Mulley, 16 March 1981, in the House of Commons where he now serves as a Member of Parliament and with Herr Georg Leber, 17 March 1981, in Bonn. The analysis is mine.

2. See *Aviation Week and Space Technology* (21 March 1977), p. 20.

3. Several German officials whom I interviewed offered this assessment. Leber himself said it would take time to bring his generals around on NATO AWACS. (See an interview with Leber by Adalbert Weinstein in the *Frankfurter Allgemeine Zeitung*, 23 December 1976, p. 1.)

4. Mulley asserted during an interview on 16 March 1981 that the United Kingdom could have agreed to another delay in deciding between NATO AWACS and Nimrod if Germany would have agreed to a share of, say, at least 20 percent. Leber, when asked to comment on Mulley's assertion, said if that were true, why didn't Mulley say so at the time?

5. Interview with Dr. Karl Schnell, 18 March 1981, who read the conditions from a document entitled, "Vortrag über das luftgestützte Radarführungssystem AWACS." Dr. Schnell presented the Vortrag to the Bundestag Defense Committee on 12 April 1978.

6. Drawn from a reporting cable, dated 26 March 1977, sent to the Departments of State and Defense by the United States Mission to NATO Headquarters. I have fleshed out the passage with information garnered from interviews with Colonels Robert Eaglet and Ed von Kospoth, both formerly with the NATO Airborne Early Warning and Control Programme Office (Provisional).

7. Sometimes, of course, ministers use meetings in the margins to discuss mutual security issues not on the agenda of the meeting.

8. Denmark's attempt to leverage issues is not a particularly unusual ploy in NATO politics and is not, therefore, the unseemly gambit it may seem to the casual observer. Denmark's coastal defense radar project qualified for infrastructure funding, but at a priority level not likely to receive a budget allocation. Trading political support for projects is a time-honored tactic practiced around the world.

9. Norway has a long-standing policy proscribing the stationing of foreign troops on Norwegian soil during peacetime. Since NATO AWACS would have multinational crews (that is, "foreign troops") Norway reserved the right to limit its operation in and around Norway.

10. NATO Press Communique M-DPC-1(77)3, dated 25 March 1977.

11. Dr. Brown is too much the gentleman and statesman to have terminated or delayed these initiatives for spite. By doing nothing to keep them going, however, he in effect allowed these first two initiatives—which different elements in the Pentagon opposed for various reasons—to atrophy. Eventually two of these three bilateral programs survived on their own merits.

12. No record now apparently exists of Ambassador Ramsbotham's letter to the Congress, but many people remember the incident. The Harrier program had hung by a thread for years, opposed by many elements in the Carter administration, but kept alive by the Congress at the urging of some elements of the US Marine Corps and the United Kingdom.

13. At about the same time, the Carter administration—principally for budgetary reasons—reduced the Air Force AWACS production rate from six to three airplanes a year. The slower production rate, among other effects, gave NATO more time to come to grips with an AWACS program.

14. The NATO staff derived the new force structure in somewhat of a backward fashion. The Programme Office

and Assistant Secretary General for Defence Support, rather than operational commanders or force structure analysts, settled on eighteen AWACS and eleven Nimrods. Their estimate of funds likely to be available played a central role in the process, as indeed it should have in light of defense ministers' guidance in June 1976.

15. NATO Press Communique M-DPC-2(77)6, 18 May 1977, numbered paragraph 17, which reads: "Ministers reviewed the status of work to develop a NATO Airborne Early Warning programme which would take into consideration the United Kingdom decision to provide its contribution in kind with Nimrod aircraft towards meeting the NATO requirement. They reaffirmed the importance of providing an Alliance-wide capability in this field through an interoperable force and agreed to devote all possible efforts to reach a decision on procurement as soon as practicable."

16. Interview with Georg Leber, 17 March 1981.

17. It is not precisely clear who was the author of the Airbus proposal. Leber was, in any event, the principal proponent of the idea.

18. Dr. LaBerge, then Assistant Secretary General for Defence Support, asked the US Air Force to estimate the cost of reengineering AWACS equipment into the Airbus. No one remembers the estimate: some said "astronomical"; another remembered it as about $300 million. Production costs would have been higher as well. And all of this begs the question whether Boeing Aerospace, prime contractor for the AWACS, would have agreed to sell at an affordable price the technical data package needed for the reengineering effort.

19. Once again, no one remembers the author of this proposal, although many remember vividly the proposal in its major particulars.

20. Concerns that the AWACS production line would close before NATO could make a decision on its program

haunted the architects of the NATO proposal. Iran's proposed purchase of AWACS had yet to be approved by Congress, and the Air Force program stood in constant danger of being axed, if for no other reason than the "fact of life" that budget cutters find $75 to $100 million airplanes owning no clearly defined mission to be attractive targets. Costs to reopen the production line would have increased rapidly over time; a six-month shutdown, for example, could have added well more than $100 million to acquisition costs.

21. Estimated fixed costs included: $160 million for Air Defense Ground Environment modifications; $70 million for basing facilities; $170 million for NATO-peculiar research and development; and $50 million for program administration.

22. Interview with Lieutenant General Wolfgang Altenburg, 17 March 1981, in Koblenz, Germany, where he served as a Corps commander. General Altenburg was the acting director of the political-military affairs office in the Central Staff during the time period under discussion. The Central Staff has no organizational counterpart in America's defense establishment. It is responsible for some of the functions of the Organization of the Joint Chiefs of Staff and some of the functions of the Office of the Secretary of Defense in the United States Department of Defense.

3. The Search for Consensus

1. Based on an interview with Lieutenant General Wolfgang Altenburg, 17 March 1981. The author attended the bilateral discussions as well.

2. Only about $75 million of the $300 million cost reduction can be attributed directly to the production efficiencies attendant to building one standardized airplane rather than two different ones. Different airplanes would require, among other things, different technical data packages, separate quality control procedures, separate accounting, and, of course, different items of equipment. The balance of the standardized AWACS cost reduction stemmed from a reduction in industrial collaboration (about $50 million), the deferral of a few NATO enhancements (about $100 million), a change in US production assumptions ($25 million), and cost benefits from the Iranian sale (about $75 million).

3. "Standardization" is one of three holy words in the lexicon of NATO political-military affairs. The descriptions that follow are not official ones (see Department of Defense directive 2010.6, dated 5 March 1980, for more precise definitions): "Rationalization" calls for governments to mesh more closely their respective defense efforts with a view toward fielding more cost-effective military forces by, for example, reducing costly duplication of effort. "Standardization," or commonality of equipment and procedures, would be close to the optimal in rational, cost-effective forces. Parts and entire systems could be interchanged among allies on the battlefield. "Interoperability" is a fallback from the optimum. If equipments are not common, they ought at least be able to operate together effectively by, for example, using common communications equipment and procedures.

4. Germany wanted high technology co-production work for the subsequent competitive advantage it might confer. Thus the standardized AWACS proposal retained German industrial collaboration on, for example, computer

software; radar equipment; avionics manufacturing, installation and checkout; and digital communications equipment.

5. See also endnote 20 in Chapter 1. Few German defense officials could bring themselves to link the two programs, perhaps because linkages can convey distasteful political implications. There are also practical reasons why linkages are a poor tactic. A worthwhile program can be jeopardized, for example, by the less worthwhile program with which it is linked—although I hasten to add this practical consideration did not play in the AWACS-tank gun linkage. Pragmatism and principle notwithstanding, a few powerful German parliamentarians held no compunctions about linkages. They pressed hard for them.

6. The United States Army's tank gun decision may itself warrant a study to sort out fact from fiction. There was an honest dispute among Army experts on whether a higher caliber (120 millimeter) round was needed to defeat new and projected Soviet armor or whether the time-honored 105 millimeter round could be improved enough to defeat the postulated threat. The 105 millimeter option enjoyed a lot of support because more rounds could be carried in a single tank. And it was a round widely used throughout the Army. The first several hundred new American main battle tanks would, in any event, be fitted with that gun because of production leadtimes. Choices, as usual, turned as much on one's assumptions as on "hard fact." Once Army seniors decided on the larger caliber (or to "up gun" in Pentagon parlance), other considerations came into play. It was politically and militarily important, for example, to salvage something from American-German failed efforts to field a common tank. Thus, there was an element of truth in many of the stories about political considerations that opponents of the decision circulated in the Army and the Congress. The vocal German parliamentarians who spoke so openly about linkages helped to ensure that the 120 millimeter gun would face stiff opposition in the Congress.

7. The Programme Office, although serving under the North Atlantic Council (as, indeed, do all NATO organizations directly or indirectly), received working level policy guidance from a multinational high level group established by the Conference of National Armaments Directors (comprised of governments' defense procurement executives). In a sense, the Programme Office answered—formally or informally—to all of these organizations and, on a daily basis, to the Assistant Secretary General for Defence Support.

8. Germany and the United Kingdom each contributed $4 million and the United States $6 million. Canada, France, and these same three governments had also provided funds for earlier study efforts and other preliminary activities. More will be said later in Chapter 4 in the section entitled, "A Precarious Beginning."

9. The Department of Defense Appropriation Authorization Act for Fiscal Year 1978, Public Law 95-79.

10. Senior positions in the International Staff are technically open to the best qualified applicants from any of the NATO governments, but have tended in historical practice to be allocated to certain governments, so as to maintain a proper mix of representation. Thus, Walter LaBerge, an American, was replaced by John Walsh, an American, who was succeeded by Vi Garber, also an American. The same tends to hold true for other Assistant Secretary General positions. Although success has many fathers, Walsh was indisputably one of a very few responsible for the success of the NATO AWACS initiative.

11. By way of background, differences in configuration (the technical details of which remain classified) were driven by different planning assumptions. The United States Air Force originally sized its AWACS computer capabilities primarily on the requirements to defend North America from a manned bomber attack, but did have plans approved to enhance those to meet more

demanding worldwide tactical requirements. NATO, on the other hand, needed an AWACS that from the outset could operate effectively in the potentially harsh environment of a central European conflict with, for example, its masses of attacking and defending airplanes.

Many people can rightfully claim credit for the standardized AWACS. The Programme Office, the prime contractor, and Pentagon officials all had a hand in the initiative. American negotiators initially resisted NATO's efforts (led by the Programme Office) to align configurations because the Air Force had neither funds nor approval for immediate changes. And the political climate of the moment suggested both would be hard to come by.

A change in circumstances, however, led to a change in the American position. The new computer, which could meet NATO's more demanding requirements, cost about the same as the older, less capable one used in the Air Force AWACS up to that point. Consequently, the United States could buy a more capable airplane at little or no price increase provided NATO would agree to fund the research and development effort needed to adapt the new computer to AWACS.

As it happened, the standardized AWACS initiative proposed by the American delegation in Bonn was not cleared through the Pentagon's staff first. It was an ad referendum proposal, actually created by the marketing organization of Boeing Aerospace, that gained support so rapidly few could have withdrawn it, had they been so inclined, without causing considerable embarrassment to the Pentagon. The standardized AWACS may be one of those rare instances of poor staff work resulting in a happy ending.

12. France wanted very much to find the first customer for the CFM-56 engine manufactured by General Electric and SNECMA of France. The engine did offer several advantages to AWACS (for example, lower fuel consumption), but the cost of re-engining the aircraft proved too

expensive for France's liking, particularly when a subscription fee (cost share in disguise) was added. The French military establishment also resisted the NATO AWACS proposition for understandable reasons. Funds would have to come from the defense budget. The French might have little to say about AWACS employment plans, and the aircraft would not be available for national contingencies in Africa or the Middle East. France rapidly lost interest in the NATO program when, according to Walsh, the DC-8 appeared on the horizon as a reengining candidate of sufficient significance to promise a successful CFM-56 program.

13. Drawn from a reporting cable of the second financial experts' meeting sent to the Departments of State and Defense on 9 October 1977 by the United States Mission to NATO Headquarters.

14. NATO's civil budget, to which all NATO governments including France and Iceland contribute, supports the administration and personnel costs of the International Staff and support personnel for NATO Headquarters.

15. Iran's order promised cost reductions for both the American and NATO AWACS programs for two basic reasons. The three programs, taken together, could have permitted the prime contractor to order components and run the production line at optimally efficient rates rather than the then inefficient rate of three units a year. Iran's order also would have spread the prime contractor's business base at some cost reduction to all three programs. Depending on assumptions, NATO's share of overall cost benefits could have amounted to as much as $75 million.

16. Subsequently, the Programme Office shifted $10 million from the German share to the Canadian share to keep their cost shares proportional to their respective industrial collaboration benefits.

17. The military budget covers the operating and support costs for NATO's various military headquarters and

headquarters' elements. All nations except Iceland contribute to the budget.

18. Drawn from a reporting cable sent to the Departments of State and Defense on 9 February 1978 by the American Embassy in Bonn, Germany.

19. The Arms Export Control Act requires the "customer" to pay actual costs.

20. Sixty percent of this sum came from German Army programs, 30 percent from German Air Force programs, and 10 percent from German Navy programs. These percentages roughly reflect the military services shares of the Federal Republic's defense budget.

21. The three nations were Denmark, Italy and Norway.

22. The $70 million cost reduction resulted from a few minor additions to and a few major subtractions from the original cost estimate of nearly $19 billion dollars. Major cost avoidances included: reductions in program management costs of about $20 million (the bulk of which would come from a waiver of certain AWACS program management costs in the Department of Defense); a price adjustment of $30 million by the contractor for aircraft production; and a $25 million reduction from a change in production assumptions concerning American AWACS (this change amounted to NATO's accepting the pricing assumptions used by the United States Government). The Programme Office's decision to publish a cost reduction of fragile substance seemed sound at the time. It may have imparted additional momentum to the program just prior to the spring 1978 ministerial meeting of the Defense Planning Committee. And it may have had a positive influence on the affordability equation in some capitals.

23. Based on an interview with General Fabio Moizo in Rome, Italy, on 19 March 1981. General Moizo is now retired from government service.

24. General Moizo related the basic story. I added details and analysis from various newspaper accounts.

25. The term "National Armaments Director" is a NATO one. Actual titles for the function vary by nation. General Moizo, for example, held the title of Secretary General of Defense.

26. The Department of Defense offered similar agreements to all NATO defense establishments in an effort to promote a more balanced defense trade between Europe and the United States—that is, to increase Europe's share. The timing of this particular offer was a fortuitous coincidence.

4. Uncertainties

1. Costs and schedule, as usual, were tied to planning assumptions. To keep costs as low as possible within the financial constraints imposed by NATO governments, the contractor planned for the first standardized AWACS (that is, the first AWACS with the new computer and software) to be an American one. NATO's first AWACS would then be the second standardized airplane. Subsequent American and NATO airplanes would alternatively come off the production line at the most cost-effective rate possible under the circumstances. For all of this to happen, NATO had to complete the research and development effort by the time specified in the contractor's assumptions.

2. A year later, the cost penalty for the late and underfunded start popped up in the contractor's formal bid price for contract negotiations. The penalty proved modest indeed: $2 million.

3. The time would have been insufficient if the decision to proceed had been a system acquisition decision where business arrangements, specifications, and other programmatic factors are paramount. Well before the spring of 1978, most knew the decision to require NATO AWACS would be a political one. That being the case, six weeks could have been more than enough time for a decision on AWACS had political costs and political benefits been in better focus.

4. The five nations included Canada, Germany, Luxembourg, the Netherlands, and the United States. The United Kingdom, not participating in the computer effort, was also scheduled to pay a share of ground environment modification costs in the first year of the program.

5. The Congress also authorized and appropriated another $10 million in fiscal year 1979 for NATO AWACS, but placed the same restrictions on its expenditure or obligation as it had on the 1978 money. The

legislative language for the 1979 money was essentially the same as it was for 1978. See endnote number 9 in Chapter 3. Observations on the technical loophole were detailed in a memorandum to the Secretary of Defense from the Office of the General Counsel, dated 9 February 1978, Subject: NATO AWACS Program—Information Memorandum.

6. The Department of Defense has three years in which to obligate monies the Congress authorizes and appropriates for research and development. Otherwise, those funds revert to the United States Treasury. In this instance (the last quarter of fiscal year 1978), the Air Force could have theoretically used fiscal year 1977 money which was not restricted in the manner of the 1978 and 1979 money. However, fiscal year 1977 money for AWACS research and development was restricted in another fashion. Anytime the Congress reduces the amount of a specific budget line item for research and development (as it had in 1977 for the US AWACS) or identifies the activity being funded as an item of congressional interest (which also applied), the Department of Defense cannot divert one cent of the money to another purpose without prior approval from the Armed Services Committee. The Air Force was spared the potential agony of seeking such approval because there was no fiscal year 1977 money left.

7. The Department of Defense Appropriation Authorization Act for Fiscal Year 1978.

8. The Nunn Amendment, Section 302(c) of Public Law 93-365, as amended by the Culver-Nunn Amendment, Section 8914 of Public Law 94-106, as amended by Section 802, Public Law 94-361, dated 14 July 1976, requires the Secretary of Defense to submit an annual written report to the Congress on progress toward the standardization of armaments in NATO. This report, known in the verbal shorthand of the Pentagon as the "Nunn Report," is a cornucopia of information on defense cooperation.

9. US Congress. Senate. Senator Nunn speaking for an unprinted amendment numbered 1404. 95th Congress, 2d Session, 11 July 1978. *Congressional Record*, Volume 12, pp. S10413-15. The Senate (and the House of Representatives, in due course) removed all legal restrictions on the $15.7 million authorized and appropriated for fiscal year 1978. However, expenditures or obligations beyond the $4.066 million requested by the Secretary of Defense required prior approval from the Chairmen of the Senate and House Armed Services Committees.

10. Defense officials asking a contractor to work when no funds are legally available could be criminally liable under the provisions of Title 31, United States Code, Section 665 (The Anti-Deficiency Act). Defense contractors, however, routinely perform work at their own expense (at their own risk) in anticipation of winning contracts.

11. The remainder of this section is based on my analysis of information provided during interviews with three German defense officials: Dr. Karl Schnell on 18 March 1981; General Altenburg on 17 March 1981; and Colonel von Kospoth on 17 March 1981.

12. The term "two-way street" has unfortunately become a political slogan. It describes the need for a more equitable balance in defense trade between the United States and its European allies. The need quite obviously was a European one. The Department of Defense acknowledged, but was hard pressed to do very much, very fast, about the gross imbalance (in favor of the United States) in military equipment purchases between Germany and the United States.

13. A German industrialist confirmed this information with a more colorful and accurate description. Schmidt, he noted, decided to pour glue on the Alliance.

14. Delays beyond the assumed 1 July 1978 starting date in the contractor's revised cost and schedule estimates for standardized AWACS required governments to begin other preparatory activities besides computer research

190 UNCERTAINTIES

and development or else jeopardize the estimates. In this instance, German industries had to invest a few million dollars of their own capital to prepare for manufacturing activities.

15. Germany's $560 million acquisition share was theoretically offset by: $240 million in industrial collaboration on NATO AWACS production; $100 million from the United States Army and Air Force procurement of nontactical vehicles (buses, forklifts, etc.) from German vendors; $95 million from the American Army purchase of an upgraded European Telephone System from the Deutsches Bundespost; $45 million from the Department of Defense for licensed production of Germany's 120 millimeter tank gun; $35 million for Germany's collaboration on modifying the NATO Air Defense Ground Environment for AWACS interoperability; and $60 million from construction activities on the AWACS main operating base at Geilenkirchen. The Federal Ministry of Defense acknowledged these sums in a written document sent on 31 October 1978 to Dr. Manfred Worner, Chairman of the Bundestag's Defense Committee. The same document pointed to DM 70 million return from Germany's annual contribution of roughly DM 60 million toward operations and support costs. Dr. Karl Schnell shared this information with me during an interview on 18 March 1981.

16. The explicit linkages sought by some German officials could have been self-defeating. The United States Congress historically has not looked kindly on deals thought up by the Department of Defense that suggest unnecessary expense for the American taxpayer. Such deals correctly remain the prerogative of the legislature.

17. The text of the Bundestag's resolution, dated 28 November 1978, approving German participation in the NATO AWACS program reads in part: "The Defense Affairs Committee requests the Federal Government (of Germany) to report on the negotiations results (for equipment purchases by the United States) prior to the

beginning of deliberations on the 1980 (German defense) budget, and, at the same time, to submit the contracts concluded (for America's purchase of German-manufactured equipment)."

18. Article in the *Frankfurter Allgemeine Zeitung* by Adalbert Weinstein on 1 December 1978.

19. The other two were the Charter for the NATO Airborne Early Warning and Control Programme Management Organization and the Acquisition Agreement between the United States and NATO. Descriptions of these documents can be found in the first two pages of Chapter 6.

20. Examples of issues resolved in this fashion included, among others: the Department of Defense agreement to seek congressional waiver for administrative surcharges; and the Department's agreement to seek legislative approval for America's contracting officers to be personally liable for mismanagement of the NATO contracts they would be administering.

21. The term "commercially sensitive" is not a security classification as such, but the effect is the same on the contractor who is denied formal access to information so labelled. The AWACS' contractor protested mildly at being denied certain details of the terms and conditions in the Memorandum, particularly those that proved difficult to implement contractually after ministers signed the document. The contractor had a point. Very little in the Memorandum fell into the category normally considered to be commercially sensitive information, such as source selection data. However, virtually all of the "imperfections" that proved difficult to implement contractually were driven by political needs.

22. The text of the Bundestag resolution, dated 28 November 1978, reads in part: "The Defense Affairs Committee assumes ... that the Federal Government (of Germany), on the occasion of the NATO Defense Planning Committee (DPC) on December 5 and 6, will link its

statement on participation (in AWACS) to the following conditions:

> "1. Waiver by the USA of:
> — the administrative charge in the amount of three percent
> — the development charge in the amount of four percent
> — the payment of personnel costs for the NATO AEW project in the US defense area (US-Verteidigungs-Bereich) ..."

This last condition required the United States to waive or absorb all incidental management costs; that is, all management costs except those incurred by the Air Force AWACS Program Office, an organization charged to negotiate and manage contracts and other acquisition activities for AWACS.

23. The Programme Office, with its staff of about 200 people, would enjoy an operating budget of $52 million over its seven-year life span. Analysts estimated 80 percent of this sum would be spent on the local economy.

24. The Charter (of the Programme Management Organization) was the relevant document. The Dutch reservation amounted to a veto on locating the Programme Office in Brussels, Belgium. Reservations, however, are less final than votes.

5. In Ministerial Session

1. This section is partly based on a reporting cable sent to the Departments of State and Defense on 5 December 1978 by the United States Mission to NATO Headquarters. I have fleshed out the passage with information gathered from interviews with staff aides and Programme Office officials who attended the session.

2. See endnote 22 to Chapter 4 for a fuller explanation of these conditions.

3. This particular condition, also contained in the Bundestag's resolution concerning German participation, came as a surprise, at least to the Americans. The condition was inconsistent with what had been an understanding on base support costs. Certain cost estimates in the Multilateral Memorandum of Understanding were predicated on the assumption AWACS would be located on an operational airfield; that is, an airfield on which other flying units were stationed. Governments participating in the NATO AWACS program would then have to fund only the increment of additional base services (for example, security, control tower operations, and fire fighting) needed to support an additional eighteen airplanes. As it happened, Geilenkirchen, Germany's candidate for the AWACS main operating base, was not an operational airfield (it did house non-flying tactical units, but they were relocated to make room for AWACS). Thus, when no defense minister objected to Apel's statement, the condition became a binding part of the agreement. (As a practical matter, objections may have delayed the program decision until governments accommodated the divergent views.) The imprecise language of the condition (one can agree in principle without actually paying; and what support activities did the Germans have in mind?) as well as the absence of advanced warning that it intended to table such a condition subsequently led to anxieties in capitals. Most governments never intended to build and support

an entire base infrastructure. In time, however, representatives reached an accommodation whereby certain nations paid some costs and Germany paid others, a problem that may have stemmed from sloppy language in the original assumption. The slice of additional funding would of course be determined by the particulars of the specific base selected, not by some vague notion of supplementing an operational base.

4. The United Kingdom's Air Defense Ground Environment (called UKADGE) was largely built with national funds. The balance of the Air Defense Ground Environment sites on the continent was largely built in roughly equal measure with common funds and national funds. (Sites on both sides of the Channel were compatible, however.) This difference, added to the uncertainty of cost estimates for ground site modifications, led Minister Mulley prudently to place a reservation on Britain's sharing of costs. Happily, the United Kingdom did eventually share some of the costs of a unified modification program.

5. General Moizo related this tale. The Committee Chairman, himself a retired military officer, apparently was predisposed to hassle Italy's defense establishment on national security issues. Consequently, the Chairman's committee colleagues frequently cast sympathy votes for Italy's defense establishment. Such are the circumstances of the unpredictable positive and negative external forces, few of which have much to do with the merits of an issue, that influence and sometimes settle decisions in NATO capitals.

6. Belgium's Minister of Defense Vanden Boeynants two years earlier had pledged funds for a share of ground environment costs. Subsequently, Belgium modified the pledge to include shares of basing and program administration costs. In May 1981, two and a half years after NATO defense ministers agreed to acquire AWACS, the

Belgian Cabinet agreed to fund its share of aircraft acquisition costs.

7. The codicils described for each country are taken from the *Multilateral Memorandum of Understanding between NATO Ministers of Defence on the NATO E-3A Cooperative Programme*. The analysis of those codicils is mine.

6. An Imperfect Agreement?

1. Article 9 of the North Atlantic Treaty, signed in Washington, DC, on 4 April 1949 by Representatives of Belgium, Canada, France, Luxembourg, the Netherlands, the United Kingdom, and United States, grants the North Atlantic Council the exclusive right to establish legally constituted subsidiary bodies of the North Atlantic Treaty Organization.

2. The idea was to weigh votes by cost shares, presumably to prevent one or two minor-share nations from insisting on actions (such as additional equipment provisions) that would cost them little and could cost the major contributors a lot. One supposes the frustration of achieving unanimity on every single course of action drove some to consider weighted votes. (The frustration is understandable, the solution is not.) Weighted or unweighted votes would make no difference unless NATO were to abandon the principle of unanimity. For fundamental political reasons NATO cannot abandon the principle of unanimity.

3. A few American defense officials complained that the Programme Office acted unfairly by adding items while simultaneously pressuring the Department of Defense to keep cost growth under control. The complaints were not entirely reasonable ones. The Programme Office did add items (each a validated requirement for which funding had previously been unavailable) that matched dollar for dollar the reduction in aircraft costs resulting from the United States waiver of certain acquisition surcharges. For example, when the Department of Defense agreed during the summer of 1978 to seek a congressional waiver for the $10 million in administrative surcharges, the Programme Office tentatively added $10 million in needed, but unfunded, capability for NATO AWACS. One might question the Programme Office's judgment for not holding the "savings" in reserve at least until the United States Air Force negotiated final prices with the Boeing Aerospace Company. However, one cannot challenge the

fairness of their actions because, for that matter, their judgment may have been sound as well. Contractors have upon occasion been known to take firmer stands during contract negotiations when they suspect the buyer enjoys some budgetary slack.

4. The additional six American AWACS provided some cost relief for the reasons discussed in endnote 15 in Chapter 3 concerning Iran's order of seven AWACS. Briefly, the additional airplanes would spread the contractor's business base and improve production efficiencies. The change in assumptions also, for better or worse, tied the cost of NATO airplanes to the health of the United States' AWACS program. Any subsequent reduction in the planned number of American AWACS, whether directed by the President or the Congress, would increase NATO's costs. The change in assumptions, although it caused great pain during the following years' battle of the budget, was, on balance, a clever move.

5. The contractor should have referred queries to the Department of Defense for political and practical reasons. Criticisms from capitals also extended to the contractor, but the bulk were aimed at the Department. The Department, therefore, should have had the sole responsibility to respond, since two conflicting answers only intensified criticism. Moreover, the contractor's bid price stood as only one portion, although the largest one, of the Defense Department's announced estimate of aircraft costs.

6. Accountants needed to reduce nations' payments to a common value in order to preserve the integrity of the cost-sharing argument. Dealing with thirteen different currencies, each with a constantly changing value relative to other currencies and a different rate of inflation (varying by sector within each economy), over a seven-year acquisition effort would be no simple task. Of course, there were different cost-sharing formulas for each of four components in the program. Basing costs were shared on the basis of NATO's infrastructure budget

formula, adjusted for twelve nations' participation. Ground environment modification costs were also shared on the basis of NATO's infrastructure budget formula, adjusted however for thirteen nations' participation (the United Kingdom was the additional contributor). Program administration costs were shared on the basis of an adjusted twelve-nation formula. Airplane acquisition costs were shared on the basis of the adjusted relative gross domestic product formula.

Adding staggered payments complicated the task immensely. Indeed, the staggered payments compromise resulted in an arrangement whereby no nation would pay its precise agreed program percentage share in any given year. Each would pay either nothing, less, or more than its share in any given year of the seven-year acquisition effort.

7. If Germany paid its agreed 30.71 percent share of program costs each year, then either its preferred inflation sharing method or the commonly preferred inflation-sharing method would have yielded identical results. Germany, however, did not enjoy the defense budget flexibility to accelerate payments to a 30.71 percent level during the early years of the program, and proposed, therefore, that the United States share with Germany the disputed sums. American defense officials did not accept the German compromise because, in constant purchasing power terms, it would have changed the agreed cost-sharing arrangements.

8. Procedures for Foreign Military Sales are prescribed in fair detail by the Arms Export Control Act. Details aside, foreign military establishments normally contract with the Department of Defense for specific defense goods or services, which, in turn, contracts with a supplier if necessary. This arrangement typically (but not always), protects both the customer (from, say, being unfairly charged by an unscrupulous supplier) and the supplier (from, for example, threats of non-payment from the customer).

200   AN IMPERFECT AGREEMENT?

Prepayment of termination liability, a protection for the supplier, is explained in endnote 29 to Chapter 1.

9. Revisions to the Arms Export Control Act, which even at the time under discussion included more liberal provisions for the member nations of NATO, have been moving toward accommodating allies' objections to being treated like just another armaments customer. The "loophole" arrangement cited here took advantage of the fact that the Arms Export Control Act permits only NATO nations to contract directly with American defense contractors, thereby avoiding the surcharges and procedures otherwise required by the Act. For the AWACS program, NATO as an entity would contract directly with Boeing Aerospace for the eighteen aircraft and also with the United States Government to negotiate and manage the direct purchase contract as well as to supply certain government furnished equipment and services. Among other advantages, this arrangement reduced the administrative surcharge from 3 percent of the purchase price for eighteen aircraft (about $1.5 billion) to 3 percent of the purchase price for Government goods and services (about $350 million).

10. Not many other Americans involved with program negotiations share this view.

SELECTED BIBLIOGRAPHY

Government Documents

United States, *Anti-Deficiency Act*, US Code, Title 31, Section 665.

Department of Defense Appropriation Authorization Act for Fiscal Year 1978, Public Law 95-79.

International Security Assistance and Arms Export Control Act of 1976, Public Law 94-329, 30 June 1976.

Congress, Senate, Senator Eagleton speaking for Amendment No. 527, 94th Congress, 1st Session, 5 June 1975, *Congressional Record* 121:17387-93.

Congress, Senate, Floor Vote on Research, Development, Test, and Evaluation Funds for the Airborne Warning and Control System, 94th Congress, 1st Session, 5 June 1975, *Congressional Record* 121:17410.

Congress, Senate, 94th Congress, 1st Session, *Congressional Record* 121:6684-5.

Congress, Senate, Senator Nunn speaking for unprinted amendment numbered 1404, 95th Congress, 2nd Session, 11 July 1978, *Congressional Record* (Daily Edition), Volume 12, pp. S10413-15.

Congress, Senate, Committee on Armed Services, *Authorizing Appropriations for Fiscal Year 1977 for Military Procurement, Research and Development, and Active Duty, Selected Reserve, and Civilian Personnel Strengths and for Other Purposes*, Report No. 94-878, 94th Congress, 2nd Session, 1976.

Congress, Senate, Committee on Armed Services, *Hearings on Fiscal Year 1978 Authorization for Military Procurement, Research and Development, and Active Duty, Selected Reserve, and Civilian Personnel Strengths*, Part 6, 2, 3, 4, 7, 8 March 1976.

Congress, House of Representatives, *Hearings Before a Subcommittee of the Committee on Appropriations*, Part I, 94th Congress, 2nd Session, 1976.

US, Congress, House of Representatives, Floor Vote on Research, Development, Test, and Evaluation Funds for the Airborne Warning and Control System, 94th Congress, 1st Session, *Congressional Record*, 121:15048-52.

Department of Defense, Directive 2010.6, 5 March 1980.

NATO, Press Communique M-DPC-2(76)17, 8 December 1976. Press Communique M-DPC-1(77)3, 25 March 1977. Press Communique M-DPC-2(77)6, 18 May 1977.

Journals, Magazines, and Newspapers

Aviation Week and Space Technology (21 March 1977): 20.

Frankfurter Allgemeine Zeitung.

Newsweek 88 (20 September 1976): 63.

Woolsey, R. James, "Systems Analysis: The Bingo Game in the Basement of the Pentagon," *Armed Forces Journal* 117 (March 1980): 35-36.

Unpublished Materials

FRG, Bundestag, Defense Affairs Committee, Resolution dated 29 November 1978.

FRG, Ministry of Defense, "Vortrag über das luftgestützte Radarführungssystem AWACS," 12 April 1978.

NATO, *Multilateral Memorandum of Understanding between NATO Ministers of Defence on the NATO E-3A Cooperative Programme*, 6 December 1978.

US, Department of State, Aide Memoire to the Government of Canada, 4 June 1976.

US Mission to NATO, cable dated 9 December 1976.

US Mission to NATO, cable dated 26 March 1977.

US Mission to NATO, cable dated 29 October 1977.

US Mission to NATO, cable dated 9 February 1978.

US Mission to NATO, cable dated 5 December 1978.

Interviews

Altenburg, Wolfgang, Lieutenant General. III Corps Commander, Koblenz, Federal Republic of Germany, 17 March 1981.

Babione, Dale. The Boeing Aerospace Company, Rosslyn, Virginia, 25 February 1981.

Eaglet, Robert D., Colonel. Air Force Systems Command, Andrews Air Force Base, Maryland.

von Kospoth, Eduoard, Colonel. (German) Air Staff, Bonn, Federal Republic of Germany, 17 March 1981.

Leber, Georg. Vice President of the Bundestag, Bonn, Federal Republic of Germany, 17 March 1981.

Moizo, Fabio, General. (Italian) Secretary General of Defense (retired), Rome, Italy, 19 March 1981.

Mulley, Frederick, Honorable. House of Commons, London, United Kingdom, 16 March 1981.

Schnell, Karl, General Doctor. (German) State Secretary for Defense (retired), Baden-Baden, Federal Republic of Germany, 18 March 1981.

INDEX

A–300 Airbus, 49, 177n17–18
Acquisition Agreement, 144, 145–46
"Action Checklist for National Positions on NATO AWACS," 117–121
Air Defense Ground Environment, 5–6, 99, 162, 165n2, 166n6, 178n21, 187n4, 194n4
Airborne Warning and Control System (AWACS), 5–13, 64
  achievements and setbacks, 161–64
  capabilities, 12, 22, 169n16
  funding arrangements, 63, 68–69, 91–93, 155. *See also* Costs; Cost sharing
  management of, 143–44. *See also* Board of Directors; Programme Management Agency; Programme Office; United States Air Force, AWACS Program Office
  numbers of, 8–9, 16, 57, 145–46, 161, 164, 167n9, 183n15, 198n4
  political considerations, 36–37, 52, 154–56. *See also* Costs; Cost sharing; specific country by name
  purpose of, 165n2
  site of main base, 59, 68, 125. *See also* Programme Office, location of AWACS main base
  Task Force, 168n11
  termination liability costs, 151–54, 199n8
Altenburg, Wolfgang, 56, 57, 58, 59, 64, 98, 178n22
Alternative proposals, 48–52, 55–56. *See also* Mixed forces; Nimrod
Anderson, John F., 19, 72, 76, 77
Apel, Mr., 97–104, 125, 126, 134–36, 151, 154–55
  and MMOU, 114–15, 116, 118
Arms Export Control Act, 26–27, 171n27, 172n31, 184n19, 199n8, 200n9. *See also* Foreign Military Sale
AWACS. *See* Airborne Warning and Control System

205

Babione, Dale, 19, 24, 27, 28, 31
Barkman, Mr., 120
Barry, John, 65
Belgium, 13, 77, 120–21
  cost sharing, 17, 52, 69–72, 73, 124, 148, 159, 194–95n6
  locating Programme Office in, 111–12, 124, 125, 131, 137
Blelloch, John, 19, 31
Board of Directors, 143–44, 149, 160–61, 162–63
Boeing Aerospace, 95, 154, 177n18, 197n3
Boverie, Richard T., 168n11
Bowman, Richard C., 64, 66, 79, 82, 86, 87
Brown, Harold, 12, 46, 87, 95, 100, 114–18, 125–31, 176n11
Brunssum. *See* The Netherlands, locating Programme Office in
Brussels. *See* Belgium, locating Programme Office in

Callaghan, James, 23
Canada, 10, 19, 38, 42, 168n12
  cost sharing, 11, 17, 38, 70, 72, 74, 127, 183n16
  funding views, 76, 77, 92, 112, 150, 151
  and MMOU, 119, 132–33
Carter, Jimmy, 15, 91
  administration, 176n12–13

Central Staff, FRG, 51–52, 178n22. *See also* Altenburg, Wolfgang
CMF–56, 182–83n12
Computer technology, 91–93, 181–82n11, 187n4, 189n14
Congress, U.S. *See also* Cost sharing, United States; Senate Armed Services Committee; Senate-House Conference Committee; United States, AWACS costs
  defense appropriations, FY78, 9, 93–94
  defense appropriations, FY79, 94–95, 187n5
  and the Harrier program, 176n12
  interim funding for NATO AWACS, 92–96
  and R&D appropriations, 188n6
  and standardization of armaments, 188n8
  opposition to AWACS, 3–4, 9, 15, 166n3, 167n10, 169n18
Costs, 1–7, 13–14, 52–53, 76–78, 90–91, 171n26, 172–73n35, 177–78n20–21, 183n15, 184n22, 187n1–2, 193n3, 197n3, 198n4
Cost sharing, 9–18, 20, 25–29, 37–40, 89–90, 143–47, 197n2
  Belgium, 69–72, 73, 159. *See also under* Belgium

INDEX 207

Canada, 11, 17, 38, 70, 72, 74, 127, 183n16
current national allotments, 70–71
Denmark, 17, 39, 77, 148, 176n8
Federal Republic of Germany, 14, 15–16, 19, 20, 21–22, 27–29, 33–35, 38, 47–48, 59, 65, 66, 70, 78–81, 183n16, 184n20, 193n3
France, 17, 20, 38, 67–68, 82
Greece, 17, 20, 140
Italy, 17, 39, 75–76, 81–82, 148
The Netherlands, 11–12, 17, 72–73, 77, 110–11
Norway, 39–40, 77, 138, 148
Programme Office proposal, 73–74, 183n16
United Kingdom, 14, 19–23, 37, 38–39, 65–66, 74, 194n4
United States, 14, 19–21, 23–28, 38, 65, 70, 72, 171n28
Currie, Malcolm, 24, 171n28

D'Ambrosio, Gen., 87
Danson, Barnett, 17, 38, 42, 92, 127, 132, 133
Defense Planning Committee, 15–18, 36–43, 115, 117–121, 169n17. *See also* Multilateral Memorandum of Understanding (MMOU)
Defense Production Sharing Agreement, 11, 168n12
Denmark
and MMOU, 119, 131, 134
and costs, 17, 39, 77, 148, 176n8
Duncan, Charles, 115, 120

Eaglet, Robert, 73, 74, 83
Eagleton, Thomas, 166n3, 167n10, 169n18
Eberhard, Hans, 97
European Affairs Bureau, US Dept. of State, 114

Feyzioglu, Mr., 17
Fischbach, Marcel, 17, 39
Ford, Gerald, administration, 9
Foreign Military Sale, 152, 172n30, 199–200n8–9. *See also* Arms Export Control Act
de Freitas-Cruz, Mr., 39
France, 38–39, 48, 58, 66, 121, 164, 182–83n12
cost sharing, 17, 20, 21, 38, 67–68, 82

Garber, Vi, 181n10
Geilenkirchen, 125
Germany, Federal Republic of (FRG), 13, 41–42, 97, 183n20. *See also*

Altenburg, Wolfgang; Apel, Mr.; Leber, Georg; Padberg, Hans; Pauls, Rolf
  alternative proposals, 48–52, 55–56
  and costs, 149, 150, 151
  cost sharing. *See under* Cost sharing
  funding views, 31, 77, 91–92, 112, 155, 159
  and MMOU, 113, 118, 126–27, 134–36, 193n3
  and the U.S., 10, 56–61, 78, 81, 100–03, 180n5–6, 189n12, 190–91n15–17, 191–92n22
  and AWACS main base, 38, 125
Gilbert, Mr., 120
Glitman, Maynard, 113, 115–16, 118
Greece, 129
  cost sharing, 17, 20, 140
  and MMOU, 121, 140
Government Furnished Equipment, 171n26

Hansen, Rolf, 17, 39, 42, 126–27, 138
Hardy, Mr., 112, 116
Harrier, 23, 45, 176n11
Hawker-Siddeley, 32, 44–45
Hill-Norton, Peter, 36, 37

Independent European Planning Group, 48
International Military Staff, 62

International Security Affairs, Office of, US DOD, 51, 114
Iran, 74, 146, 177–78n20, 179n2, 183n15
Isik, Mr., 129, 139
Italy, 13, 43, 78, 148, 194n5
  cost sharing, 17, 39, 75–76, 81–82, 148
  and MMOU, 118, 128–29, 131
  and payment schedule, 84–88, 159

Jones, David C., 12–13, 166n4, 168n11

Kirca, A. Coskun, 39
Krieps, Emile, 127, 131

LaBerge, Walter B., 20, 31, 37, 64, 177n18, 181n10
Lattanzio, Vito 17, 39, 43, 48–49, 85–86
Leber, Georg, 12–13, 15, 27, 41, 56, 78, 97–101, 103, 170n19
  and the A–300 Airbus, 49, 177n17
  and Nimrod, 31–34, 35, 38, 175n4
Leòpard II, 16, 21, 22, 170n21
Low Altitude Radar System, 99
Luns, Joseph M.A.H., 16, 36, 40–41, 89, 114, 118,

123–24, 125, 126, 128, 129, 131, 169n17
Luxembourg, 17, 39, 93, 118, 127

Marconi-Elliott, 32
Matthoefer, Hans, 99–100
McGiffert, David, 56, 60, 114–15, 118, 120
Military Committee, 4, 11, 36, 47, 62, 166n5
"Minor-share" nations, 12, 40, 77, 91, 169n15, 197n2
Miquel, Mr., 17
Mixed forces, 61, 65. *See also* Nimrod, vs. AWACS
MMOU. *See* Multilateral Memorandum of Understanding (MMOU)
Moizo, Fabio, 82, 86–87
Moore, William C., 168n11
Mulley, Frederick, 16, 31–35, 35–36, 37–38, 38–39, 40–41, 42, 43–44, 45, 74, 115, 120, 127–28, 175n4, 194n4
Multilateral Memorandum of Understanding (MMOU), 104–21, 124, 143, 149–50, 191n21, 193n3
  and ministerial session, Dec 78, 125–41
Multi-Role Combat-Aircraft, 23

NATO. *See* North Atlantic Treaty Organization (NATO)
NATO Military Committee. *See* Military Committee
The Netherlands, 10, 11–12, 17, 39, 110–11
  and costs, 70, 77, 93
  location of Programme Office, 68, 119–20, 124–25, 128, 131, 192n24
  and MMOU, 127, 137–38
Nimrod, 31, 127
  and British industry, 32–33
  costs, 65
  origins, 7–8
  termination of, 164
  vs. AWACS, 23, 32–36, 41, 44–47, 52–53, 55–56
North Atlantic Council, 62, 143, 160, 169n17
North Atlantic Treaty Organization (NATO), 7, 89–90. *See also* Defense Planning Committee; Military Committee; Programme Office
  air defense network, 5–6, 7–8
  Airborne Early Warning Programme Office. *See* Programme Office
  alliance politics, 36, 45, 55, 58, 61–62, 93, 96–97, 150
  charter, 143–44, 160
  organization of, 62, 71, 166n5, 169n17, 181n10, 183n14, 183–84n17

210 INDEX

Norway, 39–40, 42, 176n9
 funding views, 17, 77, 138, 148
 and MMOU, 118, 127, 131, 138–39
Nunn, Sam, 94–95
Nunn Amendment, PL93-365 ("Nunn Report"), 188n8

Organization for Economic Cooperation and Development, 71

Padberg, Hans, 19, 27, 31, 48, 78–80
Pahlavi, Mohammed Reza, 146. *See also* Iran
Pauls, Rolf, 15–16
Payment schedules, 82–88, 144–51, 159, 198–99n6
Permanent Representatives, 115, 140, 169n17
Petrignani, Mr., 113, 116
Piotrowski, John, 169n16
Portugal, 17, 39, 68, 112, 113
 and MMOU, 120, 129–30, 130
Programme Management Agency, 143, 144, 160, 162
Programme Office, 62, 64, 73–74, 77–78, 81–82, 92–93, 181n7, 183n16, 192n23
 and acquisition costs, 145, 197–98n3. *See also* Costs and location of AWACS Main base, 67, 111, 119–20, 124–25, 128, 131, 137–38, 192n24
 and payments compromise, 83–84, 184n22
Pustay, John S., 168n11

Radar, 5–6, 99, 166n6. *See also* Air Defense Ground Environment
Ramsbotham, Amb., 45, 176n12
Rolls-Royce, 32
Royal Air Force, 8
Ruffini, Atilio, 82, 84, 86–88, 114–15, 128–29

dos Santos, J.A. Louriero, 115, 120, 129
Schmidt, Helmut, 16, 21, 38, 60, 97, 99–100
Schmidt-Petri, Col., 64, 72, 76
Schnell, Karl, 99, 103, 104
Scholten, Mr., 119, 124, 128, 137–38
Schroeder, Patricia, 167–68n10, 169n18
Schuurmans, Mr., 111–12, 130
Scrimgeour, David M., 67
Senate Armed Services Committee, 8, 167n9, 171n28. *See also* Congress, U.S.
Senate-House Conference Committee, 95

Shackleton Airborne Early Warning Aircraft, 8, 23, 33, 41, 167n8
Skyflash missile, 44–45
Sogaard, Mr., 119, 134
South Limburg, *See* Zuid-Limburg
Standardization, 58, 94, 179n2–4, 181–82n11, 187n1, 188n8
Stemerdink, Abraham, 39
Stennis, John, 94
Svart, Anker, 17, 39

Tank gun, 22, 60, 102, 107n21, 180n5–6, 190n15
Tenassi, Mario, 85
Turkey, 17, 39
  and MMOU, 119, 129, 131, 139
"Two-Way Street," 100, 189n12

United Kingdom, 167n8, 194n4. *See also* Mulley, Frederick
  and AWACS, 7–8, 9, 37–38, 40–41, 177n15
  cost sharing. *See under* Cost sharing
  and Defense Planning Committee, 19–21, 22–23, 33–34, 43–44
  and MMOU, 120, 127–28
United States. *See also* Babione, Dale; Brown, Harold; Congress, U.S.
  AWACS costs, 24–25, 57–59, 91–96, 149, 150, 151, 171n25–26, 171n28, 172n31, 181–82n11, 183n15, 197n3, 198n4
  cost sharing. *See under* Cost sharing
  and the Defense Planning Committee, 19–21, 23–25, 26, 27, 28
  Dept. of Defense (DOD), 51, 93–94. *See also* Cost sharing, United States; and *above* costs
  as contracting agent, 69, 191n20–21, 191–92n22
  General Accounting Office (GAO), 3, 172n32
  and MMOU, 106, 108–10, 113–18
  and Germany, 10, 51–52, 56–61, 66, 78, 81, 100–03, 170n21, 179n4, 180n5–6, 190–91n17, 191–92n22
  NATO AWACS campaign, 7, 8–13, 168n11, 188n6
United States Air Force. *See also* United States, AWACS costs
  AWACS Program Office, 191n20–21, 191–92n22
  NATO AWACS campaign, 9–13, 168n11, 188n6
United States Army, 180n6
United States Marine Corps, 176n12

212 INDEX

Vanden Boeynants, Paul, 17, 39, 112, 121, 194n6
Vredeling, Mr., 17

Walsh, John B., 64, 66, 67, 73, 84, 95, 140, 181n10
  computer-funding proposal, 91, 92–93

Wehrkunde Conference, 31, 34

XM–1, 170n21

Zuid-Limburg, 125, 138

ABOUT THE AUTHOR

Colonel Arnold Lee Tessmer, United States Air Force, is a graduate of the University of Buffalo and holds a Master of Arts degree in geography from the University of Washington. During his career he served in a broad variety of assignments, ranging from operations to several key staff positions in the Pentagon. The former included tours in a Bomb Wing and Tactical Fighter Wing as well as in special operations. His Pentagon assignments were in the Air Staff (Policy Plans), Office of the Secretary of Defense (International Security Affairs), and Office of the Secretary of the Air Force (Acquisition Management). He also served in the Supreme Headquarters Allied Powers Europe. In 1980, Colonel Tessmer was selected to be a Senior Fellow at the National Defense University, Washington, DC, during which time he wrote this book. While a Senior Fellow, he also attended the National War College. Colonel Tessmer has recently retired from active service and is now employed as Marketing Manager with the Santa Barbara Research Center, in Santa Barbara, California.

POLITICS of COMPROMISE:
NATO and AWACS

Text and display lines composed in Baskerville type
Book design by Donald Schmoldt
Cover mechanical prepared by Rhonda Story

NDU Press Editor: Donald Schmoldt
Editorial Clerk: Carolyn Valentine